Psychoanalytic Treatment in Adults

T0347387

The outcomes of psychoanalysis, as with other psychotherapies, vary considerably. *Psychoanalytic Treatment in Adults* examines the results of a longitudinal study of change during psychoanalysis, illuminating the characteristics of patients, analysts, and analyses which can help to predict outcomes of treatment.

Written by two experienced psychologist psychoanalysts, chapters in the book describe longitudinal changes in sixty completed analyses to consider what patients with very different analytic outcomes were like at the beginning and end of psychoanalyses. Psychoanalysts used a clinician report measure, the Shedler–Westen Assessment Procedure, to describe a patient at the beginning of psychoanalysis and every six months until the analysis ended. This allowed the authors to learn about the prediction of analytic outcomes. An applied mathematician then considered the relationship between changes in insight and changes in other characteristics of patients ending analysis with maximum benefits.

Chapters explore five outcomes: a negative therapeutic reaction; attrition when the patient drops out; attrition due to external events; mutual agreement between patient and analyst without maximum benefits; and mutual agreement between patient and analyst with maximum benefits.

The findings from these chapters will be of interest to researchers and academics in the fields of psychoanalysis, psychotherapy, psychodynamic therapy, psychoanalytic education, psychiatry, and psychology. The results should also help clinicians recognize potential problems early in analytic treatments so that they can work more effectively with patients.

Rosemary Cogan is Professor of Psychology in the Department of Psychological Sciences, Texas Tech University, USA.

John H. Porcerelli is Director of Behavioral Medicine and Professor in the Department of Family Medicine and Public Health Sciences, Wayne State University School of Medicine, USA.

Psychoanalytic Explorations series

Psychoanalytic Treatment in Adults

A longitudinal study of change

Rosemary Cogan and
John H. Porcerelli

LONDON AND NEW YORK

First published 2016 by Routledge

2 Park Square, Milton Park, Abingdon, Oxfordshire OX14 4RN
711 Third Avenue, New York, NY 10017

Routledge is an imprint of the Taylor & Francis Group, an informa business

First issued in paperback 2017

Copyright © 2016 Rosemary Cogan and John H. Porcerelli

The right of Rosemary Cogan and John H. Porcerelli to be identified
as authors of this work has been asserted by them in accordance
with sections 77 and 78 of the Copyright, Designs and Patents Act
1988.

All rights reserved. No part of this book may be reprinted or reproduced or
utilised in any form or by any electronic, mechanical, or other means, now
known or hereafter invented, including photocopying and recording, or in
any information storage or retrieval system, without permission in writing
from the publishers.

Notice:
Product or corporate names may be trademarks or registered trademarks,
and are used only for identification and explanation without intent to infringe.

British Library Cataloguing in Publication Data
A catalogue record for this book is available from the British Library

Library of Congress Cataloging in Publication Data
Cogan, Rosemary, author.
Psychoanalytic treatment in adults : a longitudinal study of change /
Rosemary Cogan and John H. Porcerelli.
p. ; cm. — (Psychoanalytic explorations)
Includes bibliographical references and index.
I. Porcerelli, John H., 1957- , author. II. Title. III. Series:
Psychoanalytic explorations series.
[DNLM: 1. Mental Disorders—therapy—Case Reports.
2. Psychoanalytic Therapy—Case Reports. 3. Longitudinal Studies—
Case Reports. 4. Treatment Outcome—Case Reports. WM 460.6]
RC480.5
616.89'1—dc23
2015033271

ISBN: 978-1-138-90258-9 (hbk)
ISBN: 978-0-8153-5986-9 (pbk)

Typeset in Bembo
by Swales & Willis Ltd, Exeter, Devon, UK

Contents

PART III
Insight and change   **125**

PART IV
Conclusions   **141**

Preface

We met some years ago when we were each in a training year at Detroit Psychiatric Institute Hospital. We both cherished clinical work, psychoanalytic theory, and research. Rosemary returned to the faculty in the Department of Psychological Sciences at Texas Tech University and was in clinical practice for many years. John went to the Department of Family Medicine at Wayne State University School of Medicine and is also in clinical practice. Our collaboration and friendship continued at a distance as we both completed psychoanalytic training at the Dallas and Michigan Psychoanalytic Institutes respectively.

We are deeply grateful for the patient, careful work of the participating analysts that made this longitudinal study possible. We are grateful as well to the International Psychoanalytical Association, which provided important funding for this project as it began. We thank Drew Westen and Jonathan Shedler for sharing their measure, the Shedler–Westen Assessment Procedure, and for discussions with us about the measure and this project.

We thank Brian Quinn and others on the faculty and staff of the Texas Tech University Library for their outstanding help throughout this work. We thank Kathy Gillis, our superb writing consultant at Texas Tech University; we have watched our writing improve because of her help.

We thank our families and friends who encouraged this work. Finally, we thank analysts past, present, and future.

Introduction

Three longstanding questions have led to this work. First, what characteristics of patients at the beginning of analysis predict different outcomes of analysis? To answer this question required a longitudinal study. Second, what characterizes patients at the end of analyses that have ended with different outcomes in the view of analysts? What, for instance, differentiates between patients who end analysis with *maximum benefits* in contrast to patients who end analysis with *good* outcomes but *without* maximum benefits? These questions have really not been answered in the wealth of psychoanalytic clinical and research literature. Finally, we wanted to know more about how change occurs in analysis. The development of the Shedler–Westen Assessment Procedure (SWAP: Shedler, 2015; Westen & Shedler, 1999a, 1999b) made this longitudinal study possible.

The SWAP, a clinician report measure, includes 200 items that might describe a person. The items were developed over some years and are worded in theory-neutral language that can be agreed on by all sorts of clinicians with widely varying perspectives. The clinician sorts the items into eight categories ranging from those that describe the patient very well to those that are irrelevant, do not apply to the patient, or about which nothing is known by the clinician, with a fixed number of items required in each category. From this, individual items or groups of items can be used to describe an individual patient or group of patients; scales of personality disorders, traits, and adaptive functioning can also be used to describe patients. The SWAP was grounded in extensive research and further empirical support for the measure developed rapidly after the measure became available. We tested the measure ourselves in several preliminary studies (Cogan, 2007; Cogan & Porcerelli, 2005; Porcerelli, Cogan, & Hibbard, 2004). Satisfied with the results, we set to work on the longitudinal study of change during psychoanalysis that is the subject of this book. A SWAP Insight scale was later developed by Lehmann and Hilsenroth (2011) and we have included this with the original SWAP scales.

As we begin, in Chapter 1 we consider the beginnings of psychoanalysis itself. The first of the "talking therapies" began when Joseph Breuer, a prominent Viennese physician, met once and then twice a day with his patient Anna O. Psychoanalysis developed as Breuer and Freud met and contemplated this interesting and complicated case. Questions about understanding the outcome of a case began even in this first case. We then consider the literature on the goals of psychoanalysis and the goals of psychotherapy.

In Chapter 2, we organize a review of the empirical literature on the outcomes of psychoanalysis, which began with Coriat's work in 1917. For our review, we use the template developed by Wallerstein (1995).This template includes first-generation studies which are retrospective and have the analyst as the assessor, second-generation studies which are studies with independent judges of outcome, and third-generation studies which are prospective and include contemporary international studies.

In Chapter 3, we describe the background of our longitudinal project. We describe the development of the SWAP-200 (Westen & Shedler, 1999a, 1999b), which provides a clinically grounded, reliable and valid clinician report measure of pathological and healthy dimensions of personality. The SWAP-200 provides a measure that has been used in idiographic and nomothetic studies, as well as in longitudinal case studies of psychoanalytic outcome. We describe how we recruited analysts for this longitudinal study. We describe the analyses at the beginning, including descriptions of the analysts, the analysands, and the analyses. There are some unique features to our descriptions, interesting in their own right. Just as at the beginning of any talking therapy, the picture at the beginning is only a background for what will develop.

A primary purpose of this longitudinal study was to identify characteristics at the beginning of analysis that predict the eventual outcome of analysis. This long-term prediction will help analysts maximize patients' gains from analysis. After describing characteristics of the patient, analyst, and analysis every 6 months from the beginning to the end of analysis, as each analysis ended, the analyst identified the analysis as having ended in one of five different ways. A few analyses ended with a negative therapeutic reaction, with a serious worsening of the patient's problems. More than a few analyses ended with attrition, either when the patient dropped out of analysis or when the analysis was interrupted because of external events. Analyses also ended with the mutual agreement between analyst and patient either with or without maximum benefits. We describe what patients were like at the end of analyses with the different outcomes.

In Chapter 5, we consider analyses ending with a negative therapeutic reaction. We compare these analyses with all of the other analyses in the project at the beginning and end of analysis. We then consider analyses ending with attrition. We compare analyses ending when the patient dropped out with all of the other analyses. In Chapter 6, we compare analyses ending because of external events with all of the other analyses. We continue in Chapter 7 by directly comparing analyses in the two attrition groups to understand more about similarities and differences between analyses in which the patient drops out and analyses which end because of external events. Our goals in the three chapters on attrition have to do with being able to predict dropping out and endings from external events as the analyses began and to understand how patients in the two attrition groups differ from other patients as the analyses end. In the direct comparison of the two attrition groups in Chapter 7, we are able to more closely understand similarities and differences between these two attrition groups at the beginning and end of analysis. Predicting attrition has practical usefulness. The close comparison helps to make clear the extent to which the two attrition groups are really different.

We continue by considering analyses ending with the mutual agreement of analyst and patient. In Chapter 8, we compare analyses ending with mutual agreement but without maximum benefits in the view of the analyst and all of the other analyses. In Chapter 9, we compare analyses ending with mutual agreement and with maximum benefits and all of the other analyses. We continue in Chapter 10 by directly comparing analyses in the two groups ending with mutual agreement between analyst and patient with and without maximum benefits at the beginning and end of analysis. Our goals in the three chapters on endings with mutual agreement are to be able to predict the two endings from characteristics at the beginning of analysis and to understand similarities and differences between the two groups at the end of analysis.

Chapter 11 is unique in studies of change during psychoanalysis and psychotherapy. Naturally occurring mental health treatments vary greatly in length. Certainly the length of psychoanalysis varies widely. Special mathematical techniques are required to understand changes over the course of treatments that vary extensively in duration. In Chapter 11, with an applied mathematician co-author, we employ special techniques in applied mathematics to understand the relationships between important variables in treatments of widely varying lengths. The mathematical work sheds light on two important problems. First, we explore the relationship between changes in insight and changes in dimensions of adaptive functioning, personality disorders, and personality traits. Second, we use these modeling procedures to quantify the relative duration of the three phases of psychoanalysis (the initial, middle, and termination phases). This is the beginning of a new type of inquiry necessary to understand change during psychoanalyses and is the beginning of a new kind of collaboration between psychoanalysts and applied mathematicians.

Chapter 12 is a summary of what we have learned from the longitudinal study. Perhaps most importantly, we learned that we can understand important aspects of psychoanalytic outcomes, including negative therapeutic reactions, dropouts, and endings with patient and analyst agreement with and without maximum benefits. It was unexpected to us, and perhaps will be to the reader, that these predictions of outcomes turned out to be quite good with SWAP-200 items alone describing the analysands as the analyses began. We were not surprised to learn that we could not predict endings from external events but this confirmed for us that this is, indeed, an outcome of analysis. As has probably been the case with readers, we had expected to find a relationship between insight and change during psychoanalysis. We had not expected that the picture of changes in insight during psychoanalysis would shed light on both the role of insight and on the length of phases of psychoanalysis.

We think that the findings will be useful in practice and in further research. Finally, we also believe that a well-developed and well-researched clinician report measure such as the SWAP has a tremendous amount to offer in research in psychoanalysis and psychotherapy, in clinical practice, and in training the next generation of psychoanalysts and psychotherapists.

References

Cogan, R. (2007). Therapeutic aims and outcomes of psychoanalysis. *Psychoanalytic Psychology, 24*, 193–207.

Cogan, R., & Porcerelli, J. H. (2005). Clinician reports of personality pathology of patients beginning and ending psychoanalysis. *Psychology and Psychotherapy: Theory, Research and Practice, 85*, 36–47.

Coriat, I. H. (1917). Some statistical results of the psychoanalytic treatment of the psychoneuroses. *Psychoanalytic Review, 4*, 209–216.

Lehmann, M. E., & Hilsenroth, M. J. (2011). Evaluating psychological insight in a clinical sample using the Shedler–Westen Assessment Procedure. *The Journal of Nervous and Mental Disease, 199(5)*, 354–359.

Porcerelli, J. H., Cogan, R., & Hibbard, S. (2004). Personality characteristics of partner violent men: A Q-sort approach. *Journal of Personality Disorders, 18(2)*, 151–162.

Shedler, J. (2015). Integrating clinical and empirical perspectives on personality: The Shedler–Westen Assessment Procedure (SWAP). In S. K. Huprich (Ed.), *Personality disorders: Toward theoretical and empirical integration in diagnosis and assessment*. Washington, DC: American Psychological Association, pp. 225–252.

Wallerstein, R. S. (1995). *The talking cures: The psychoanalyses and the psychotherapies*. New Haven: Yale University Press.

Westen, D., & Shedler, J. (1999a). Revising and assessing Axis II, Part I: Developing a clinically and empirically valid assessment method. *American Journal of Psychiatry, 156(2)*, 258–272.

Westen, D., & Shedler, J. (1999b). Revising and assessing Axis II, Part II: Toward an empirically based and clinically useful classification of personality disorders. *American Journal of Psychiatry, 156(2)*, 273–285.

Part I

Beginnings

Chapter 1

Therapeutic aims of psychoanalysis

> There are people of spirit and there are people of passion, both less common than one might think. Much rarer are the people of spirit and passion. But the rarest is passion of the spirit. Bertha Pappenheim was a woman of passion of the spirit . . . Hand on this image. Hand on her memory. Be witness that it still exists. We have a pledge.
>
> Martin Buber (cited in Edinger, 1963/1968)

Introduction

The patient was a young woman with a powerful intellect, great common sense, and tenacious will-power, sometimes reaching obstinacy (Breuer & Freud, 1893/1981). When her father became critically ill, she devoted herself to caring for him at night while her mother cared for him during the day. After 5 months of this work, challenging at both an emotional and a physical level, the young woman developed several increasingly serious health problems and became bedridden. The family physician, Joseph Breuer, was called to check on her cough, which was especially worrisome as her father was dying of tuberculosis. Breuer saw the patient on December 11, 1880, and recognized that she had hysteria, with a whole host of widely varying symptoms well beyond a simple cough (Breuer & Freud, 1893/1981; Hirschmüller, 1978). Breuer began to visit her once a day and they talked together each day for about half an hour. After a few months, he began using hypnosis, asking her to talk about the development of one symptom during each visit. He found that when the history of the symptom became clear, the symptom itself eased. The patient spoke of the treatment as the "talking cure" (and sometimes as "chimney sweeping"). However, new and disturbing symptoms continued to develop. At times parts of her body were paralyzed. She had problems with her vision. At one point, she saw her fingers as snakes. At another time, she could not drink from a glass. For some time, she could not speak her native German but could only speak other languages. After about a year, as symptoms continued to develop, Breuer came to talk with her twice a day for about 30 minutes of conversation each time for several months. Her father died on April 5, 1881, and about 10 days later the prominent psychiatrist, Richard von Krafft-Ebing, was also consulted to see about the young woman's continuing health problems. Breuer continued his treatment, the symptoms eased, and the treatment ended with the mutual agreement of patient and doctor on June 7, 1882 (Loentz, 2007; Orr-Andrawes, 1987). The patient was "free from the innumerable disturbances which she had previously exhibited," although "it was a considerable time before she regained her mental balance entirely" (Breuer & Freud, 1893/1981, pp. 40–41). Breuer later described the young woman as gifted, energetic, and kind (Breuer & Freud, 1893/1981). However, Breuer never used the cathartic method again (Hirschmüller, 1978).

We know this patient as Anna O., the pseudonym given to her in writings about the case. Her identity was disclosed by Ernest Jones in 1953 and was then confirmed in letters and medical records (Ellenberger, 1972). Her given name was Bertha Pappenheim. She was the oldest living daughter born to a wealthy orthodox Jewish family in Vienna on February 27, 1859 (Hirschmüller, 1978). After her father died and her treatment with Joseph Breuer came to an end in June, 1882, she was in a sanatorium from July 12, 1882 to October 29, 1882, where she was treated for a dependency on morphine and chloral hydrate, medications given to her to treat a cough, sleep, and pain problems (Ellenberger, 1972; Hirschmüller, 1978; Orr-Andrawes, 1987). By 1887 she had been treated four more times in a sanatorium (Orr-Andrawes, 1987). She moved from Vienna to Frankfurt in November, 1888. After several years, about which little is known, she recovered and blossomed. From 1895 to the end of her life she worked with devotion and skill as the director of a girls' orphanage for refugees from Eastern Europe, as a social worker, as a feminist activist, and as a well-published writer (de Paula Ramos, 2003; Ellenberger, 1970; Freeman, 1972/1990; Kimball, 2000; Loentz, 2007; Orr-Andrawes, 1987; Rosenbaum & Munroff, 1984). She lived from February 27, 1859, to May 28, 1936 and was honored for her social welfare work in 1954 when the West German Republic issued a postage stamp recognizing her in a series on Benefactors of Mankind (Jensen, 1970).

Breuer talked with his young Viennese colleague, Sigmund Freud, about the treatment of Bertha Pappenheim on November 18, 1882 (Freeman, 1972/1990; Strachey, 1981) and again on July 13, 1883 (Hirschmüller, 1978). Breuer and Freud knew each other from the community and from the Institute of Physiology, where both had worked with the physician and physiologist Ernst Brücke at different times. Freud had become engaged to Martha Bernays in June, 1882, and was preparing to move from research with Brücke to private practice in order to be able to afford to marry. As part of Freud's preparation for practice, from October 20, 1885 to February 23, 1886, he studied with the famous neurologist Jean-Martin Charcot, who was working with hypnosis as a treatment for hysteria at the Salpêtrière Hospital in Paris. Although Charcot's use of hypnosis was not exactly a "talking therapy," his use of hypnosis was part of developing ideas about hysteria and how it could be treated.

Freud returned to Vienna and began his medical practice in late April, 1886. Freud and Martha married on September 30, 1886, and he and Breuer continued to collaborate. Freud worked first with hypnosis and then turned to a "talking therapy" without hypnosis. The case of Anna O. is described in the first sections of *Studies on Hysteria* (Breuer & Freud, 1893/1981), which introduced the core ideas of the "cathartic method," as it was conceptualized at the time. The complete version of the work, with the histories of Anna O. and four cases treated by Freud, with a fifth case described briefly in a footnote, was published in 1895. Although the case of Anna O. is an important and much studied and debated case in the pre-history of psychoanalysis, perhaps what matters most for us here is that, in an addendum to the case, Freud (1903/1981) ends the last section of *Studies on Hysteria* with the famous statement about the goals of treatment:

> much will be gained if we succeed in transforming your hysterical misery into common unhappiness. With a mental life that has been restored to health you will be better armed against that unhappiness.
>
> (p. 305)

Goals of psychoanalysis and psychotherapy

Goals of psychoanalysis

One of the challenges of considering outcomes of psychoanalysis is differentiating between goals having to do with changes in the structure of the mind, goals having to do with changes in the analytic process, and therapeutic goals. Balint (1936) has described the first of these – focusing on structural changes – as the "classical" group of descriptions and the second – focusing on dynamic and emotional factors – as the "romantic" group.

Analytic goals having to do with changes in the structure of the mind derive from Freud. Freud wrote of helping to make "the unconscious accessible to consciousness" (e.g., 1903/1981, p. 253), with the patient having "rather less that is unconscious and rather more that is conscious in him than he had before" (1917, p. 435). In 1933, Freud considered that the goal of analysis is:

> to strengthen the ego, to make it more independent of the superego, to widen its field of perception and enlarge its organization so that it can appropriate new portions of the id.
>
> (p. 80)

Analytic goals having to do with dynamic changes, often called process goals, center around the patient's ability to free-associate. The development of an analytic process certainly may be related to changes in the structure and dynamics of the mind (cf. Jones, 1936/1961) and to therapeutic outcomes (Bachrach, Weber, & Solomon, 1985). Balint (1936) has described the ability of patients late in analysis to express wishes that had been out of awareness and to then be able to move toward gratification of these wishes as a "new beginning." In Balint's view, these newly recognized wishes involve pleasurable activities and are "without exception, directed towards objects" (p. 210). Balint observed that late in analysis an ability to form real relationships develops and the person is able not simply to *be loved* but to "attempt to begin *to love* anew" (p. 216). The development of insight has been considered as a necessary part of the process of change by both "classical" and "romantic" psychoanalytic thinkers (cf. Jacobs, 2001, 2004; Kris, 1956; Wallerstein, 1965; Weinshel & Renik, 1992) and may be a necessary precursor to other changes (Weinshel & Renik, 1992).

We do not mean to entirely set aside the extensive and thoughtful literature having to do with structural and dynamic goals of analysis. However, we are concerned here with what are generally called therapeutic goals (cf., Jones, 1936/1961; Sandler & Dreher, 1996; Wallerstein, 1965, 1992). These may include both clinical goals, such as reducing anxiety, and life goals, such as achieving a better quality of life (Bernardi, 2001; Kogan, 1996). If we can assume that symptoms are often more transient and elements of personality structure more stable characteristics of people, we might be concerned with both symptom reduction and changes in personality characteristics with analysis.

The classical psychoanalysts were generally quite cautious about the therapeutic goals of treatment. We have noted Freud's (1903/1981) comment above about achieving "common unhappiness" as a goal. Hartmann (1939, p. 311) wrote that "a healthy person must have the capacity to suffer and to be depressed." Knight (1941, p. 437) pointed to the success of analysis in terms of symptomatic recovery, improved productiveness, improved sexual pleasure, more loyal interpersonal relationships, and enough insight to manage the conflicts of daily life. However, Knight then cautioned:

> It is an entirely illogical and unfair expectation for the patient, his friends, relatives or referring physician to anticipate that after being treated by the method of psychoanalysis he will become a paragon of all the virtues and accomplished without flaw, defect or anxiety and capable of behaving in every possible situation like a superman. . . . One might as well expect that psychoanalysis would also cure his freckles, his bad golf swing and his aversion to turnips. No, the patient will remain essentially the same person after the best analysis – rid of his disabling symptoms, perhaps, or able to handle what ones are still left, more adaptable, more productive, happier in his relationships, but still the same person as to native endowment, appearance, and basic temperament.

On the more positive side, Freud and Breuer viewed the relief of symptoms as a goal of treatment, along with the restoration of the patient's ability to work (Breuer & Freud, 1893/1981). In 1904, Freud wrote of the patient's ability to lead an active life and have a capacity for enjoyment as goals of analysis. Freud wrote as well, in letters to Putnam, that analysis should "find a place among the methods whose aim is to bring about the highest ethical and intellectual development of the individual" (letter of March 30, 1914 in Hale, 1971) and Blass (2003) has considered ethical dimensions of psychoanalytic goals. Jones (1936/1961) said that with analytical success at the highest degree: "One may then expect a confident serenity, a freedom from anxiety, a control over the full resources of the personality that can be obtained in no other way than by the most complete analysis possible" (p. 382).

Statements about the therapeutic goals of psychoanalysis have varied quite a lot. Some examples of statements about therapeutic goals, organized chronologically, are: an active life, experience enjoyment, reduction in symptoms (Freud, 1904); increased sexual pleasure (Balint, 1932; 1952); confident serenity with freedom from anxiety (Jones, 1936/1961); less sadism, more love (Balint, 1936); able to tolerate suffering and depression and freedom from symptoms (Hartmann, 1939); able to handle ordinary problems, symptomatic recovery, increased productiveness, increased sexual pleasure, improved interpersonal relationships, and insight (Knight, 1941); self-acceptance and self-understanding (Glueck, 1960); to love and work (Wallerstein, 1965); personal life goals (Ticho, 1972); professional life goals (Ticho, 1972); and insight (Grinberg, 1980; Weinshel & Renik, 1992).

Goals of psychotherapy

Articulating the goals of psychotherapy is also complicated. After client-centered therapy, Rogers (1951) noted that people "feel more comfortable with themselves. Their behavior changes, often in the direction of better adjustment" (p. 131). With cognitive therapy, Beck (1976) said that people can "create a more self-fulfilling life" (p. 4), and "maintain their equilibrium most of the time" (p. 14). Generally, though, the goal of cognitive therapy is to "alleviate the overt symptoms or behavior problems" (Beck, 1976, p. 321). In behavior therapy, treatment goals are individualized for the patient with the more general goals involving changing habits in order to remove suffering or improve functioning (Wolpe, 1967, 1969). In "rational therapy," Ellis saw the goals as having the patient minimize anxiety and hostility (Ellis, 1967).

In the tour-de-force meta-analysis of 475 controlled studies of psychotherapy outcome by Smith, Glass, and Miller (1980), the researchers identified 12 outcome categories and listed from three to 43 measures of each. The outcome categories included: addiction, emotional-somatic complaints, fear-anxiety, global adjustment, life adjustment, personality traits, physiological measures of stress, self-esteem, social behavior, sociopathic behavior, vocational-personal development, and work/school achievement.

Conclusion

We confess to being at something of a loss. If each of the therapeutic goals of psychoanalysis and each of the goals of psychotherapy were written on cards and then the cards were shuffled, we doubt that the cards could be successfully sorted into one set for psychoanalysis and one set for psychotherapy. While we might expect the goals of the two types of treatments to be similar, we would surely also expect differences. Perhaps nobody – whether psychoanalyst or psychotherapist – would feel that maximum benefits of treatment had been reached if the person *never* experienced enjoyment or *often* had fear-anxiety at the end of treatment. Each of us would have ideas about what "an active life" or "life adjustment" means. On the other hand, surely nobody would expect psychoanalysis or psychotherapy to lead to *always* experiencing enjoyment or *never* experiencing fear or anxiety.

While our purpose in this longitudinal study of change during psychoanalysis is not to compare the outcomes of psychoanalysis and psychotherapy, we think the descriptions of therapeutic goals are far from clear in either case, as we have shown above. One of our objectives in our longitudinal study has been to learn more about the characteristics of patients identified by psychoanalysts as having completed analysis with maximum benefits, with clear descriptions of characteristics that have been developed and tested in the context of research. The descriptions will provide a new kind of information about the goals of psychoanalysis by learning the views of contemporary psychoanalysts about exactly what patients ending analyses with maximum benefits may be like.

The amazing case of Anna O. can alert us to some cautions. When her treatment ended, with the mutual agreement of doctor and patient, Anna O. seems to have been very much improved. Her symptoms evidently eased. She was articulate and she and Breuer reached an agreement about the ending of the treatment. It is also clear that, during the next few years, her troubles were certainly not at an end. Five periods of time in sanatoriums is not trivial in terms of treatments indicating that she had problems. The problems seem to have had to do with recovery from an addiction to morphine and chloral hydrate, given for physical treatment of a limited range of health problems and not the shifting and very dramatic range of symptoms involved in Breuer's treatment. Not being able to drink from a glass, for instance – just one example of a symptom of Anna O.'s which disappeared with Breuer's treatment – is scarcely going to involve a health problem in the usual sense of the term.

Anna O.'s extraordinary life from the age of 29 might well lead us to a view of her "talking cure" as having been a remarkable help to Bertha Pappenheim. Certainly Breuer's treatment was not psychoanalysis as it would be developed just a few years later. Perhaps the reader will join us in considering how we might each assess the therapeutic outcome of Breuer's treatment of Anna O. Was it a negative therapeutic reaction? She did, after all, spend time in sanatoriums after the treatment ended. Certainly Anna O. did not drop out of treatment. Given that Anna O. and Breuer – even though this was a treatment that came before psychoanalysis proper developed, let us call them the patient and the analyst – mutually agreed to end the treatment, we might then ask whether this was an ending with or without maximum benefits. We confess to being deeply impressed by Bertha Pappenheim's accomplishments and by the integrity, kindness, devotion to helping others, hard work, and productivity she showed throughout her life. We have never personally known anyone recognized by having a postage stamp with her picture on it.

References

Bachrach, H. M., Weber, J. J., & Solomon, M. (1985). Factors associated with the outcome of psychoanalysis (clinical and methodological considerations): Report of the Columbia Psychoanalytic Center Research Project (IV). *International Review of Psycho-Analysis, 12,* 379–388.

Balint, M. (1932). Character analysis and new beginning. In M. Balint (Ed.), *Primary love and psycho-analytic technique.* New York: Liveright, pp. 159–173. (Reprinted in 1952.)

Balint, M. (1936). The final goals of psycho-analytic treatment. *International Journal of Psychoanalysis, 7,* 206–216.

Beck, A. T. (1976). *Cognitive therapy and the emotional disorder.* New York: International Universities Press.

Bernardi, R. (2001). Psychoanalytic goals: New and old paradoxes. *Psychoanalytic Quarterly, 70,* 67–98.

Blass, R. B. (2003). On ethical issues at the foundation of the debate over the goals of psychoanalysis. *International Journal of Psychoanalysis, 84,* 929–943.

Breuer, J., & Freud, S. (1893). Studies on hysteria. In J. Strachey (Ed. and transl.), *The standard edition of the complete psychological works of Sigmund Freud* (Vol. 2). (Reprinted in 1981.)

de Paula Ramos, S. (2003). Revisiting Anna O.: A case of chemical dependence. *History of Psychology 6(3),* 239–250.

Edinger, D. (1968). *Bertha Pappenheim: Freud's Anna O.* Highland Park, IL: Congregation Solel. (Original German language edition 1963, Frankfurt: Ner-Tamid-Verlag.)

Ellenberger, H. F. (1970). *The discovery of the unconscious: The history and evolution of dynamic psychiatry.* New York: Basic Books.

Ellenberger, H. F. (1972). The story of Anna O.: A critical review with new data. *Journal of the History of the Behavioral Sciences, 8(3),* 267–279.

Ellis, A. (1967). Goals of psychotherapy. In A. R. Mahrer (Ed.), *The goals of psychotherapy.* New York: Appleton-Century-Crofts, pp. 206–220.

Freeman, L. (1972). *The story of Anna O.: The woman who led Freud to psychoanalysis.* New York: Paragon House. (Reprinted in 1990.)

Freud, S. (1895). The psychotherapy of hysteria. In J. Strachey (Ed. and transl.), *The standard edition of the complete psychological works of Sigmund Freud* (Vol. 2). London: Hogarth Press, pp. 253–305. (Reprinted in 1981.)

Freud, S. (1903). Fragment of an analysis of a case of hysteria. Postscript. In J. Strachey (Ed. and transl.), *The standard edition of the complete psychological works of Sigmund Freud* (Vol. 7). London: Hogarth Press, pp. 1–122. (Reprinted in 1981.)

Freud, S. (1904). Freud's psychoanalytic procedure. In J. Strachey (Ed. and transl.), *The standard edition of the complete psychological works of Sigmund Freud* (Vol. 17). London: Hogarth Press, pp. 249–254). (Reprinted in 1981.)

Freud, S. (1917). Mourning and melancholia. In J. Strachey (Ed. and transl.), *The standard edition of the complete psychological works of Sigmund Freud* (Vol. 15). London: Hogarth Press, pp. 237–258. (Reprinted in 1981.)

Freud, S. (1933). New introductory lectures on psycho-analysis. In J. Strachey (Ed. and transl.), *The standard edition of the complete psychological works of Sigmund Freud* (Vol. 22). London: Hogarth Press. (Reprinted in 1981.)

Glueck, B. (1960). Psychoanalysis: Reactions and comments. In P. H. Hoch & J. Zubin (Eds.), *Current approaches to psychoanalysis*. New York: Grune & Stratton, pp. 123–140.

Grinberg, L. (1980). The closing phase of the psychoanalytic treatment of adults and the goals of psychoanalysis: 'The search for truth about one's self'. *International Journal of Psychoanalysis, 61*, 25–37.

Hale, N. G. Jr. (Ed. and transl.) (1971). *James Jackson Putnam and psychoanalysis: Letters between Putnam and Sigmund Freud, Ernest Jones, William James, Sandor Ferenczi, and Morton Price, 1877–1917*. Cambridge, MA: Harvard University Press.

Hartmann, H. (1939). Psychoanalysis and the concept of health. *International Journal of Psychoanalysis, 20*, 308–321.

Hirschmüller, A. (1978). *The life and work of Josef Breuer: Physiology and psychoanalysis*. New York: New York University Press.

Jacobs, T. J. (2001). Reflections on the goals of psychoanalysis, the psychoanalytic process, and the process of change. *Psychoanalytic Quarterly, 40*, 149–181.

Jacobs, T. J. (2004). Life changes, analytic changes revisited: Current perspectives on their relationship. *Journal of the American Psychoanalytic Association, 52(4)*, 1025–1040.

Jensen, E. M. (1970). Anna O – A study of her later life. *Psychoanalytic Quarterly, 39*, 269–273.

Jones, E. (1936). The criteria of success in treatment. In Jones, E. *Papers on Psychoanalysis*. Boston: Beacon Press (pp. 379–383). (Reprinted in 1961.)

Kimball, M. M. (2000). From "Anna O." to Bertha Pappenheim: Transforming private pain into public action. *History of Psychology, 3(1)*, 20–43.

Knight, R. P. (1941). Evaluation of the results of psychoanalytic therapy. *American Journal of Psychiatry, 98*, 434–446.

Kogan, I. (1996). Termination and the problem of analytic goals: Patient and analyst, different perspectives. *International Journal of Psychoanalysis, 77*, 1013–1029.

Kris, E. (1956). On some vicissitudes of insight in psycho-analysis. *International Journal of Psychoanalysis, 37*, 445–455.

Loentz, E. (2007). *Let me continue to speak the truth: Bertha Pappenheim as author and activist*. Jerusalem, Israel: Hebrew Union College Press.

Orr-Andrawes, A. (1987). The case of Anna O.: A neuropsychiatric perspective. *Journal of the American Psychoanalytic Association, 35(2)*, 387–419.

Rogers, C. (1951). *Client-centered therapy*. Cambridge, MA: Riverside Press.

Rosenbaum, M., & Munroff, M. (1984). *Anna O: Fourteen contemporary reinterpretations*. New York: Free Press.

Sandler, J., & Dreher, A. U. (1996). *What do psychoanalysts want? The problem of aims in psycho-analytic therapy*. New York: Routledge.

Smith, M. L., Glass, G. V., & Miller, T. I. (1980). *The benefits of psychotherapy*. Baltimore: Johns Hopkins University Press.

Strachey, A. (1981). Editor's introduction to *Studies on Hysteria (1893–1895)*. In J. Strachey (Ed. and transl.), *The standard edition of the complete psychological works of Sigmund Freud* (Vol. 2). London: Hogarth Press, pp. x–xxx.

Ticho, E. A. (1972). Termination of psychoanalysis: Treatment goals, life goals. *The Psychoanalytic Quarterly, 51*, 315–333.

Wallerstein, R. S. (1965). The goals of psychoanalysis: A survey of analytic viewpoints. *Journal of the American Psychoanalytic Association, 13*, 748–770.

Wallerstein, R. S. (1992). The goals of psychoanalysis reconsidered. In A. Sugarman, R. Nemiroff, & D. Greenson (Eds.), *The technique and practice of psychoanalysis 2. A memorial volume to Ralph R. Greenson.* Madison, CT: International Universities Press, pp. 63–90.

Weinshel, E. M., & Renik, O. (1992). Treatment goals in psychoanalysis. In A. Sugarman, R. Nemiroff, & D. Greenson (Eds.), *The technique and practice of psychoanalysis. 2. A memorial volume to Ralph R. Greenson.* Madison, CT: International Universities Press, pp. 91–99.

Wolpe, J. (1967). Behavior therapy and psychotherapeutic goals. In A. R. Mahrer (Ed.), *The goals of psychotherapy.* New York: Appleton-Century-Crofts, pp. 129–144.

Wolpe, J. (1969). *The practice of behavior therapy.* New York: Pergamon.

Chapter 2

Research on psychoanalytic outcomes

if the personality illness were judged really slight . . . , I would regard the indication for psychoanalysis as very seriously in doubt . . . a simpler, less intensive form of psychotherapy may suffice for many such illnesses.

(Stone, 1954)

Introduction

At some level, every analysis begins with hope. In a perfect world, a well-trained analyst begins to work with a suffering patient well motivated for change. Since we are considering psychoanalysis proper rather than any other form of therapy, the two meet and talk several or many days of the week for several years until, eventually, the analysis ends. In this perfect world, the ending is orderly and the patient's suffering has eased.

There are complications in the real world. We might wonder who the analysts are and who the people are who begin analysis. We would certainly observe right away that sometimes analyses are interrupted, and sometimes analyses proceed to a planned and orderly termination. We would notice that outcomes differ by any perspective we might consider. In the real world, our central questions would probably be how to predict how the analysis will end, how to predict the patient's well-being at the end of the analysis, and how the new information might be useful in analytic work.

The clinical literature considering all of this is extensive, thought provoking, and useful. At times the clinical literature is inspiring and lovely; at times it is simply opaque. Our concern here is with the research literature. Even rigorous and enthusiastic empiricists are likely to agree that the research literature can be less lovely and more arduous to read than the clinical literature, for all sorts of reasons. Further, empirical work is never beyond criticism. The hope that empirical research offers is to test our ideas about the world so that we can set aside ideas that are not supported by careful observations. Empirical findings can also lead us to new ideas, to new hypotheses that we might test another time. The research literature on analysts, analysands, and the outcomes of analysis is considerable. Our intent here is to review the quantitative empirical research literature related to our search for understanding endings and change during psychoanalysis. We will consider only work with adult outpatients and we will primarily consider work written in English.

Wallerstein (1995) has conceptualized research in psychoanalysis in four groups, of which three relate to our work. The *first-generation* studies are groups of outcome reports, usually with the analyst as the assessor and usually retrospective. The *second-generation* studies include prospective studies with aggregated data, often from psychoanalytic treatment centers, with independent judges and some kind of describable criteria. The *third-generation* studies include outcome studies, including intensive longitudinal study of individual cases. The *fourth-generation* studies are psychoanalytic process studies; these are not directly relevant to the present work, and will not be considered here.

The studies

"First-generation" studies

The earliest investigators of psychoanalytic outcomes braved the issues that remain important today. Diagnoses, parameters of treatment, and relevant outcome dimensions each received attention in these retrospective reviews of groups of analyses, with the outcome assessments generally made by the treating analyst. The eight major first-generation studies include Coriat (1917); a group of five studies reviewed by Knight (1941) with data from Berlin, London, Chicago, New York, and the Menninger Clinic; an American Psychoanalytic Association project (Hamburg et al., 1967); and the Southern California Psychoanalytic Institute Clinic (Feldman, 1968). These studies span more than 50 years and are organized chronologically here.

Coriat

The first-generation studies began with Coriat's (1917) report of the outcomes of the analyses of 93 of his patients "in which a complete psychoanalysis was done" (p. 210). Coriat practiced in Boston. He considered the outcomes of patients in 13 diagnostic categories. He considered that 78% of his patients had recovered or were much improved in response to analyses lasting a month for mild cases and 4–6 months for people with severe problems. Coriat concluded that hysterias, compulsion neuroses, and sexual neuroses were particularly responsive to psychoanalysis.

Berlin, London, Chicago, New York, and Menninger

Knight (1941) summarized the results of data from Berlin (1926–1930; 592 patients; Fenichel), London (1926–1936; 74 patients; Jones), Chicago (1932–1937;

157 patients; Alexander), New York (1933–1936; 29 of 43 [diagnosable] patients included), and Menninger (1932–1941; 100 patients). Knight recognized five criteria for measuring the success of analysis: symptomatic recovery, increased productiveness, improved adjustment to and pleasure in sexual life, improved interpersonal relationships, and sufficient insight to handle ordinary conflicts and reasonable reality stresses. Thirty-one percent of treatments were "broken off," a lively name for what is called "premature terminations" in contemporary language. Premature terminations were most common among people with psychoses or organic conditions. When psychoanalysis lasted for 6 months or longer, people with psychoneuroses, character disorders, or organ neurosis – including a dozen different disorders ranging from peptic ulcers to bronchial asthma and essential hypertension – were very likely to have responded well to treatment. On the other hand, of people with psychoses, only 25% were much improved or cured with psychoanalysis. Knight reported also that 15% of people in analysis for 6 months or longer had no change or were worse. Problematic reactions were most common among people with psychoses.

American Psychoanalytic Association

The report of this line of endeavors (Hamburg et al., 1967) is very much a cautionary tale. The American Psychoanalytic Association established committees in 1952, 1957, and 1961 to pool data on psychoanalytic outcomes. Members of the American Psychoanalytic Association were each given 25 sets of questionnaire sheets and asked to complete and return one for each patient in treatment and another when the patient left treatment.

Patients were identified only with a code number so the identity of the patients was confidential. About 10,000 initial reports were completed in the mid-1950s. Along the way, each committee realized that the questionnaire and approach had insurmountable methodological problems. The reports were made at very different lengths of time in analysis. There were problems with the questions about diagnosis and judgments of treatment outcome. Outcome reports could very well have been returned selectively. A considerable amount of data had been lost or discarded. Still, data from 3,019 questionnaires had been entered into the database and the committee reported on some of the information from 2,983 of these reports, including 1,490 reports of patients in psychoanalysis and 1,529 reports of patients in psychotherapy. More patients completed psychoanalysis than completed psychotherapy (57% vs. 37%). Psychoanalysis was reported as effective more often than psychotherapy.

Perhaps the most important aspect of the final report (Hamburg et al., 1967) was the recommendations for future work: Studies should have a clear purpose, an individual or office managing the project and data, systemized procedures, and clear assessments of change. A fifth recommendation had to do with issues about questionnaire responses and keypunching, reminding us that the ways of working with data change over time.

Southern California Psychoanalytic Institute Clinic

Last in the first-generation studies is a report from the Southern California Psychoanalytic Institute Clinic (Feldman, 1968). The patients considered in the report were among 120 selected from 960 applicants for analysis and the 99 analyses were of adults whose analyses were not too brief and whose records were reasonably complete. The analysts were candidates in psychoanalytic training. The data came from case records and from the analysts' ratings of cases in the previous 2 years. Most of the patients were still in analysis at the time of the report, with an average of 300–400 hours in treatment (range 160–1,000 hours). The analyses were viewed as having very good or good analytic outcomes at the point of assessment by 64% of the evaluating analysts and by 79% of the analysts who were candidates.

"Second-generation" studies

The first-generation studies helped clarify some of the problems of research on psychoanalytic outcomes. Some of the complexities were considered at psychoanalytic meetings and published papers (cf. Cheney & Landis, 1935; Kubie, 1952, Kubie & Brenner, 1949; Miles, Barrabee, & Finesinger, 1951; Rapaport, 1968). Out of these discussions came the second generation in Wallerstein's (1995) conceptualization, with consideration of completed analyses with formal assessments of diagnosis and change made by independent judges rather than by the analyst only. The four major second-generation studies considered below, in chronological order, include studies of aggregated data from the Columbia Psychoanalytic Center, Boston Psychoanalytic Institute, the New York Psychoanalytic Institute and, finally, the German Psychoanalytical Association (DPV) study.

Columbia University Center for Psychoanalytic Training and Research

Bachrach (1995) has told the story of the Columbia Records Project, which still contains "the largest number of psychoanalytic cases collected in the world!" (Bachrach, 1995, p. 280). The clinic was founded in 1945 and the project officially began in 1959.

The major reports of the Columbia work include two sets of data. The first set includes information about 588 patients in psychoanalysis and 760 in psychodynamic therapy treated at the Treatment Center between 1945 and 1962 (Bachrach, 1995; Bachrach, Weber, & Solomon, 1985; Weber, Bachrach, & Solomon, 1985a, 1985b; Weber, Solomon, & Bachrach, 1985). The treatments were carried out by candidates in psychoanalytic training. The data were from clinic records assessed by a team of experienced analysts and from questionnaires completed by the treating analyst. The records included measures of 34 patient and 16 analyst characteristics. The outcome measures concerned the circumstances of termination and ratings on scales in five areas that were also reported at the start of analysis. The analyst rated the outcomes of analyses that continued after the student analyst graduated. The first set of data included complete data available for 295 patients in analysis and 286 patients in psychodynamic therapy. The second set of data included information about 112 patients in analysis and 125 patients in psychodynamic therapy at the Treatment Center between 1962 and 1971. In the second set, the data were from clinic records, the analyst, and questionnaires completed by patients. In both sets of data, the patients in psychoanalysis were highly selected based on intake interviews. About 10% of applicants were accepted, chosen for psychological strengths. Candidates in psychoanalytic training treated the patients and the data included only patients seen for more than six sessions. Understanding of the outcomes of the analyses is complicated by the fact that, when the analyst graduated, generally, when the patient had been in analysis for less than 2 years, some patients continued the analysis and some did not. Sometimes, for instance, analyses were interrupted when the analyst graduated and left the city. When the analyst remained in the city, some patients continued in psychoanalysis and others moved from psychoanalysis to psychotherapy.

In the first sample, analyses most often lasted for 4 or more years (65%) and psychotherapy most often lasted for less than 2 years (96%). Patients were viewed as much improved or improved more often in psychoanalysis (69%) than in psychotherapy (56%: Weber, Bachrach, & Solomon, 1985a). In the second sample, the analyses most often lasted for 2–4 years (42%) and psychotherapy most often lasted for less than 2 years (96%). As in the first sample, patients were viewed as much improved or improved more often in psychoanalysis (96%) than in psychotherapy (79%: Weber, Bachrach, & Solomon, 1985b). In both samples, patients at the beginning of psychoanalysis were viewed as functioning at higher levels than patients at the beginning of psychotherapy. Patients who continued psychoanalysis when their analyst graduated were most often viewed as much improved or improved (91%), while those who ended their analysis when their analyst graduated or who were in psychotherapy were less often improved or much improved (56%). The most consistent finding about the outcome of analysis was that the treatment length was related to the outcome of psychoanalysis with a correlation of 0.46 ($p < 0.05$) between the treatment length and rated improvement in the analyses that continued to a natural conclusion rather than ending when the student analyst graduated and left the clinic. In the second sample, which included patient reports at the end of treatment in the clinic, patients were almost all very satisfied or satisfied with their treatments in psychoanalysis (100%) or psychotherapy (90%).

Boston Psychoanalytic Institute

The Boston studies included 183 patients who began analysis at the Boston Psychoanalytic Institute between 1959 and 1966 (Sashin, Eldred, & Van Amerongen, 1975). Three raters independently reviewed the detailed materials in the initial assessments to screen potential analysands and completed a 103-item questionnaire for each case. In 1966, a questionnaire about the outcome of the analyses was sent to each of the 66 analysts. Forty-nine analysts responded and described 130 of the 183 cases. The average length of treatment was 675 hours (range 100–1,760 hours) and the analyses had ended an average of 3 months earlier (range 24–133 months). The analysts at the beginning of the analyses were in psychoanalytic training. Ninety analyses had ended with mutual agreement between patient and analyst. Analyses that ended with mutual agreement between patient and analyst had the most improvement in global functioning and had the longest treatment length, except for a small group whose analyses became "interminable."

New York Psychoanalytic Institute

The New York studies included two groups of analyses (Erle, 1979). The first group included 40 consecutive patients who began analysis at the Treatment Center of the New York Psychoanalytic Institute between 1967 and 1969. The Treatment Center sample was highly selective, with the 40 patients who began analysis selected from 870 who applied for analysis (4.6%), based on a series of interviews. At the beginning of treatment, the analysts were in analytic training. The analyses were followed up at intervals from 1971 to 1977 and included assessments by the analysts and questionnaire responses from patients. The analyses were generally five times a week, although sometimes the frequency was four times a week in the last year of lengthy analyses. The analyses of 71% of the patients continued for more than 2 years and 25% continued for more than 5 years. Many of the cases ended prematurely, for instance, when the analyst graduated and left the Treatment Center. The analysts viewed 60% of the analyses as having good outcomes. Although the research team also sent patients follow-up questionnaires, only 17 of the 40 patients responded. Only the length of treatment was related to the outcome of analysis. The second group of analyses included 42 patients seen in private practice by experienced analysts from 1984 to 1989 and followed prospectively. Twenty-five of the 42 analyses had ended at the time of the report. Of the 25, the analysts viewed six (24%) as having had substantial benefit and 19 (76%) as having terminated prematurely.

Erle and Goldberg (1984, 2003) continued their work and reported on two groups of analysis. The first study involved analysts' retrospective reports of the analyses of 161 patients they saw in private practice from 1973 to 1977. Half of the patients were in analysis for 4–8 years. The analysts viewed 74% of the outcomes as good to excellent. Patients whose analyses were longer had good to excellent outcomes more often than patients whose analyses were shorter. The second study involved analysts' prospective reports of the analyses of 92 patients they saw in private practice from 1984 to 1989. Half of the patients were in analysis for 2–7 years (the median for terminated cases was 4 years). The analysts viewed 66% of the outcomes as good to excellent.

German DPV Study

The DPV study was a naturalistic study of patients whose treatments lasted at least 1 year and ended between 1990 and 1993 (Beutel & Rasting, 2002; Leuzinger-Bohleber & Target, 2002; Leuzinger-Bohleber, Stuhr, Ruger, & Beutel, 2003; Ruger, 2002). In 1992, the DPV formed a research committee which surveyed the 774 members of the DPV in 1997 to test the feasibility of a naturalistic follow-up study of psychoanalytic treatments. Eighty-nine percent of the DPV members supported the idea of the study and the group sent surveys to the analysts. In response, 207 were willing to participate in the next part of the work and 114 were not. Overall, the analysts considered the global outcome of 2,179 treatments completed between 1990 and 1993 and rated 59% of the outcomes of treatment as very good or good. The outcome assessments of analysts willing and analysts not willing to involve former patients in further assessments did not differ. Of the 453 patients contacted, 401 agree to take part in the study. Of these, two samples of people who had been in treatment for at least 1 year and were not training or teaching cases were randomly selected. One sample was asked to complete several questionnaires and 154 of 207 patients responded (84 were in psychoanalysis, with three or more sessions a week, and 123 were in psychodynamic therapy, with one or two sessions a week). A second sample was invited to complete two follow-up interviews by a member of the research group, and 129 of 194 participated (123 in psychoanalysis and 71 in psychodynamic therapy). An analyst from a different city than their own interviewed the patients. In the second group, a member of the research group who had no other information about the patient also interviewed the treating analyst. Finally, for 47 complete cases, health care utilization information was also collected from health insurance companies. The analysts were experienced, with an average of 13 years of experience since graduation from analytic training. The treatments had continued for about 4 years and had ended, on the average, 6.5 years before the follow-ups. The ratings of patients in psychoanalysis and those in psychodynamic therapy did not differ on a five-point scale of satisfaction with their treatments, ranging from very satisfied to very dissatisfied, and most (75.9%) were either satisfied or very satisfied with their treatments. Four to six percent of patients in the interview sample treatments had very negative outcomes in the view of the former patient and/or analyst. Similarly, the ratings of analysts in the two groups did not differ and most (66.2%) were either satisfied or very satisfied with the therapeutic outcomes. The researchers reported that there were no consistent differences in the outcome measures (including outcome ratings, responses to the Symptom Checklist-90-Revised [SCL-90-R], and a measure of life satisfaction) of patients who had been in psychoanalysis and patients who had been in psychotherapy. Health insurance records showed that people took fewer days of sick leave after treatment than they had before treatment. Beutel and Rasting (2002) note: "We do not intend to compare their effectiveness [because] this is not feasible in a retrospective design" (p. 130).

"Third-generation" studies

Third-generation studies involve prospective work and assessments by someone other than the treating analyst. This line of work began with the Psychotherapy Research Project (PRP) at the Menninger Foundation and what are called the newer Boston studies. More recently, third-generation studies involve patients in large cities or whole countries. These include the Heidelberg–Berlin, Helsinki, Netherlands, Munich, and Stockholm studies. Several other studies are under way. We have arranged the studies in the early and more recent lines of research alphabetically for ease of reading.

Early third-generation studies

THE PSYCHOTHERAPY RESEARCH PROJECT

The PRP of the Menninger Foundation (Kernberg et al., 1972; Wallerstein, 1986[1]) continued from 1954 to 1982. After a 4-year screening period, 42 patients who had come to the Menninger Foundation for treatment began psychoanalysis or psychotherapy based on clinical considerations. The project ultimately compared changes in 22 patients in psychoanalysis and 20 in intensive psychotherapy, with intensive clinical materials, including psychological assessment data, providing data throughout. Treatments ranged from 7 months to 10 years and follow-up interviews were 2 years to more than 23 years after the end of treatment. The analysts were candidates in psychoanalytic training. Wallerstein (1986) concluded that psychoanalytic treatments included more supportive elements and psychotherapy more analytic elements than might be expected and that about 60% of patients in both treatments improved. Eleven of the 22 psychoanalytic patients had problems or conditions that would rule out psychoanalysis in many settings (e.g., alcoholism, drug addiction, paranoia) and 6 of these had to be moved to psychotherapy. Ego strength at the beginning of treatment was related to the outcome of treatment. Luborsky's Health Sickness Rating Scale – the basis for the Global Assessment of Functioning Scale (GAF) in DSM-III-R and DSM-IV (American Psychiatric Association, 1980, 1994) – came from this study (Luborsky, 1962). Wallerstein (1986) concluded that psychoanalysis was problematic for patients who would now be identified as presenting with borderline or narcissistic personality disorders. Several people have reanalyzed the data. In one reanalysis, Blatt (Blatt, 1992; Blatt & Shahar, 2004) found that anaclitic patients (who have more interpersonal concerns) did better in psychotherapy and patients with introjective defenses (who have more concerns with identity and self-worth) did better in psychoanalysis.

THE NEWER BOSTON STUDIES

In a prospective, longitudinal study, Kantrowitz and colleagues studied 22 patients in psychoanalysis. The patients were carefully interviewed and screened by members of the Boston Psychoanalytic Institute and completed psychological assessments before beginning analysis. The analysts were candidates in psychoanalytic training. The analyses were four to five times a week and lasted from 2.5 to 9 years (Kantrowitz, Paolitto, Sashin, Solomon, & Katz, 1986). One year after the end of analysis, each patient completed psychological tests and a follow-up interview. A member of the research group also interviewed each analyst. Two people on the research team independently reviewed and rated the test and interview data blind to whether the psychological test and interview data had been collected before or after analysis. Affect availability and tolerance increased after analysis and painful affects decreased (Kantrowitz et al., 1986). After analysis, the level and quality of object relations and interpersonal relationships also improved (Kantrowitz, Katz, Paolitto, Sashin, & Solomon, 1987a). Reality testing was unchanged at the end of analysis (Kantrowitz, Katz, Paolitto, Sashin, & Solomon, 1987b). Finally, a member of the research group interviewed 17 patients 5–10 years after the end of analysis. Of the 17 patients, seven had improved, six had deteriorated but had improved after more treatment, and four had deteriorated. The research group could not predict the stability of changes (Kantrowitz, Katz, & Paolitto, 1990a, 1990b). The group thought that something about the match between the patient and the analyst was important in analytic outcomes (Kantrowitz, 1986; Kantrowitz et al., 1989; Kantrowitz, Katz, & Paolitto, 1990c).

Later third-generation studies

HEIDELBERG–BERLIN STUDY ON LONG-TERM PSYCHOANALYTIC THERAPIES

Analysts in private practice in Heidelberg and Berlin participated in the Heidelberg–Berlin prospective naturalistic study, which began in 1997 (Grande et al., 2006, 2009). Each analyst was invited to include one consecutive psychoanalytic and one psychodynamic therapy case in the study. Patients ($N = 76$) were included if they completed preliminary interviews and questionnaires and if they agreed to, and did, begin treatment. The measures the patients completed included the Global Severity Index of the SCL-90-R and a measure of relationship problems, the Inventory of Interpersonal Problems (IIP). The patients in the two groups were carefully matched for demographic and other characteristics and had at least moderately severe disorders, rated by independent reviewers based on videotaped Operationalized Psychodynamic Diagnostic interviews (OPD Task Force, 2001). Eight of the 40 patients who began psychoanalysis and six of the patients who began psychodynamic therapy dropped out of treatment. Five additional patients continued treatment but withdrew from the research project. For three more patients, the treatments were modified so extensively that their data were excluded. Finally, then, 32 patients were in psychoanalysis, with three or more sessions a week for an average of 44.2 months (SD = 14.3 months) and at least 150 sessions. Twenty-seven patients were in psychodynamic therapy once a week for an average of 24.2 months (SD = 25.5 months). Psychoanalysis was more effective than psychodynamic therapy in terms of reducing the Global Severity Index and IIP scores at the end of treatment and at 1-year (Grande et al., 2006) and 3-year follow-ups (Grande et al., 2009), and the effect sizes were large. Structural changes at the end of therapy predicted 3-year outcome evaluations by the patients better than symptomatic changes.

HELSINKI STUDY (KNEKT ET AL., 2011)

Between 1994 and 2000, patients in the Helsinki region with longstanding problems with anxiety or mood disorders were recruited for a quasi-randomized study (Knekt et al, 2011, 2012). Of 506 prospective patients, 139 refused to participate. Of the 326 who were willing to participate, patients were randomly assigned to solution-focused therapy (one session every 2 or 3 weeks for up to 12 sessions; N = 97), short-term psychodynamic psychotherapy (one session a week for 20 sessions; N = 101), or long-term psychodynamic psychotherapy (two or three sessions a week for approximately 3 years; N = 128). Forty-one patients self-selected for psychoanalysis. At the beginning of the treatments, the patients beginning psychoanalysis had more education, fewer used psychotropic medication, and the patients were more motivated for treatment than patients beginning psychotherapy. The groups did not differ in more than two dozen other characteristics, ranging from age to symptoms. Some patients refused participation (N = 34) and 47 discontinued treatment prematurely. Some patients were lost to follow-up. The average length of therapy ranged from 9.8 sessions in 7.5 months (SD = 3.0) for the solution-focused therapy, 18.5 sessions in 5.7 months (SD = 1.3) for the short-term dynamic psychotherapy, 232 sessions in 31.3 months (SD = 11.9) for the long-term dynamic psychotherapy, and 646 sessions in 56.3 months (SD = 21.3 months) for psychoanalysis. Slightly more than half of the patients also received some auxiliary therapy, most often medication. Auxiliary therapies were less frequent in the psychoanalytic group.

The patients were followed for 5 years (Knekt et al., 2012), with ten measurement blocks, with self-report measures of depression, anxiety, symptoms, work ability, and psychological functioning, and four interviews. Follow-ups are planned for 5 more years. The short-term therapies produced a faster reduction in symptoms than psychoanalysis but, by the 5-year follow-up period, patients in psychoanalysis had more reduction in symptoms and psychoanalysis was more effective than psychotherapy in reducing symptoms and improving work ability.

MUNICH PSYCHOTHERAPY STUDY

This prospective research project was started in 1995 after therapists approached researchers for help in assessing their practices (Huber, Henrich, Gastner, &

Klug, 2012; Huber, Klug, & von Rad, 2002). Patients with a primary diagnosis of major or recurrent depression seeking treatment at the Clinic for Psychosomatic Medicine and Psychotherapy, Technical University, Munich, were randomly assigned to psychoanalysis ($N = 35$) or psychoanalytic therapy ($N = 31$). A cognitive-behavioral group was added later ($N = 34$). Psychoanalysis included three or more sessions a week on the couch for an average of 234 sessions (range 17–370 sessions) over an average of 39 months (range = 3–91 months). Psychoanalytic therapy included one session a week for an average of 88 sessions (range 12–313 sessions) over an average of 34 months (range = 3–108 months). Cognitive-behavioral treatment included one session a week for an average of 44 sessions (range = 7–100 sessions) over 26 months (range = 2–78 months). The 21 therapists had graduated from approved psychoanalytic institutes and were experienced. Two of the six researchers had a cognitive-behavioral orientation.

Measures at intake included assessments of two videotaped intake interviews and additional measures completed by patients and therapists. The therapists audiotaped every session and provided basic information about each session. Patients and therapists completed self-report measures before treatment, at the end of treatment, and 1 year after the end of treatment. Patients were interviewed at the end of treatment and at a 1-year follow-up. The measures completed by the patients included the Beck Depression Inventory (BDI), the SCL-90-R, a short form of the Inventory of Interpersonal Problems, and (to measure potential mediators) the INTREX Introject Questionnaire and the Helping Alliance Questionnaire, patient form. Measures completed by the therapists include the Helping Alliance Questionnaire, Therapeutic Attitude Questionnaire, and questions about diagnosis. Patients and therapists completed additional measures twice a year. The researchers are also collecting follow-up data 2 and 3 years after termination.

Measures of symptoms showed pre–post treatment improvements in all three groups, with no differences between the groups. Interpersonal problems did not change in response to cognitive-behavioral therapy, were reduced with psychodynamic therapy, and were reduced most with psychoanalysis (Klug, Filipiak, & Huber, 2012). Process measures completed twice a year for patients in the psychoanalytic and psychodynamic therapy groups and every 3 months for patients in the cognitive-behavioral group showed that positive introjects, as measured by the Scales of Psychological Capacities scored from semi-structured interview responses, mediated changes in symptom measures (Klug et al., 2012).

THE NETHERLANDS INSTITUTE STUDY

In this quasi-experimental project with an accelerated longitudinal design, carried out from 2004 to 2007, researchers assessed change during treatment among patients in psychoanalysis (three to five times a week on the couch) or in psychoanalytic psychotherapy (once or twice a week). Each patient entered the project before treatment, 1 year into treatment, at the end of treatment, or 2 years after treatment ended. Each patient was assessed three times in 1 year. The clinicians who provided treatments were licensed and were members of one of four psychoanalytic societies in the Netherlands (Berghout & Zevalkink, 2009; Berghout, Zevalkink, Katzko, & deJong, 2012). Each patient had a minimum of 25 sessions or 1 year of treatment. The average length of treatment was 6.5 years for patients in psychoanalysis (SD = 2.7) and 3.9 years for patients in psychodynamic psychotherapy (SD = 2.5). The patients completed self-report questionnaires and interviews to assess symptoms and structural change. The measures included measures of symptoms (e.g., the SCL-90-R and BDI-II) and interpersonal difficulties (e.g., the IIP-64, and the Adult Attachment Interview). The measures also included a measure of process completed by patients and therapists (the Helping Alliance Questionnaire-II). Finally, the measures also included a measure of the cost of treatment and the costs associated with psychiatric illness and a measure of patient satisfaction. At the end of the second year of treatment, patients with psychoanalytic psychotherapy (N = 73) had reduced symptoms and reduced interpersonal problems, while patients in psychoanalysis (N = 40) had few changes (Berghout et al., 2012). Of 231 subjects, 182 completed the measures in the year before treatment began, at the end of treatment, and 2 years after treatment ended; 78 were in psychoanalysis and 104 were in psychoanalytic psychotherapy (Berghout, Zevalkink, and Hakkaart-van Roijen, 2010). Overall, psychoanalysis was more costly and was more effective in terms of improving the quality of life as compared with psychoanalytic psychotherapy (Berghout et al., 2010). The researchers raise some concern about differential attrition in this design, which is basically cross-sectional.

THE STOCKHOLM OUTCOME OF PSYCHOANALYSIS AND PSYCHOTHERAPY PROJECT (STOPPP)

The project was a three-wave panel survey of people before, during, and after psychoanalysis or psychodynamic psychotherapy in Stockholm County, Sweden. The project was started in 1992 and national health care insurance provided 3 years of subsidies for a treatment by analysts and therapists for a limited number of people (Blomberg, Lazar, & Sandell, 2001; Falkenstrom, Grant, Broberg, & Sandell, 2007; Lazar, Sandell, & Grant, J., 2006; Sandell, Blomberg, & Lazar, 2002; Sandell et al., 2000, 2006). The subsidy limitations led to long wait lists for the two treatments. The challenges of the project were formidable and are described by Sandell, Blomberg, and Lazar (1997). As one example, it turned out that many of the patients on the wait list were actually already in unsubsidized treatments.

Ultimately, data were available from 76 people in psychoanalysis three to five times a week, carried out by psychoanalysts, and 344 people in psychodynamic therapy once or twice a week, carried out by psychotherapists. The average number of sessions for patients in psychoanalysis was 3.6 sessions a week

(SD = 0.7), with an average of 642 sessions (SD = 324) over 4½ years (mean = 54 months, SD = 23). The average number of sessions for patients in psychotherapy was 233 sessions (SD = 151) over almost 4 years (mean = 46 months, SD = 24). The patients completed self-report measures once a year for 3 years. The therapists also completed questionnaires. National health insurance and health care records were examined. Twenty patients were also interviewed (Falkenstrom et al., 2007). Finally, 650 people in two non-clinical groups – a community sample and a student sample – also responded to the questionnaire completed by patients to provide normative information. Patients in both groups experienced less symptom distress and improved morale as treatment continued. In the 3 years after treatment ended, patients in psychoanalysis improved more than patients in psychotherapy. Subjective health improved with treatment but health care utilization as reported by the patients did not change.

Conclusions

There are three consistent conclusions from the literature. First, psychoanalysis is often effective (shown in all of the studies). Second, at the end of treatment, psychoanalysis is generally more effective than psychoanalytic therapy and other treatments (Heidelberg–Berlin Study; Munich Psychotherapy Study; Netherlands Institute Study). Third, the effectiveness of psychoanalysis increases after the end of analysis while the effectiveness of other treatments does not increase (Heidelberg–Berlin Study; Helsinki Study; STOPPP).

We had hoped to consider characteristics of the analysts that predict the outcomes of psychoanalysis. In the literature, however, the analysts are shadowy figures, beyond describing them as analytic candidates (e.g., Wallerstein, 1986) or members of major analytic organizations (e.g., STOPPP: Sandell et al., 2000). In the STOPPP project, the patients of female analysts had somewhat better outcomes than the patients of male analysts and the outcomes were somewhat better among older analysts (Sandell et al., 2000).

We had hoped to learn about characteristics of patients that predict the outcomes of psychoanalysis. In this area, the earlier literature provides clues. Positive predictors include hysteria, compulsions, and sexual neuroses (Coriat, 1917), sexual disorders, psychoneuroses, and character disorders (Knight, 1941), and younger patients (Hamburg et al., 1967). Negative predictors include psychoses (Knight, 1941).

We had hoped to learn about the effects of the frequency of analysis. The literature, however, includes no data in this area. We had hoped to learn about the duration of analysis. In this area, the literature includes several studies finding that longer analyses have better outcomes (Columbia studies 1 and 2; Boston; New York Psychoanalytic; Erle, 1979; Sashin et al., 1975; Weber et al., 1985a; Weber et al., 1985). However, the findings are much less clear when the problem of premature termination or dropouts is considered. In the early studies, shown most clearly in Knight's (1941) careful compilation of the Berlin, London, New York, Chicago, and early Menninger studies, 31% of treatments were "broken off." Knight (1941) did not provide information about what predicted premature termination, nor do studies that are more recent. In many of the more recent studies, longer analyses may well have had better outcomes simply because they were not terminated prematurely. To take the most extreme example, in the Columbia University Center project (Bachrach, 1995), data were only limited to patients who were in analysis for at least six sessions!

We have considerable empathy for limitations in the extant literature and cannot pretend that we have been able to resolve all of the problems. We will, however, consider how characteristics of patients and analysts in our sample at the beginning of analysis may predict how analyses end. We will consider differences in the frequency of analysis. We will learn more about predictors of deterioration during treatment and more about predictors of good vs. poor outcomes of analysis.

Note

1 As Parloff (1987) pointed out, there had been at least 68 papers about the PRP; more have been written since 1987. We have limited references to two major books about the project.

References

American Psychiatric Association. (1980). *Diagnostic and statistical manual of mental disorders* (3rd ed.). Washington, D.C.: Author.

American Psychiatric Association. (1994). *Diagnostic and statistical manual of mental disorders* (4th ed.). Washington, D.C.: Author.

Bachrach, H. M. (1995). The Columbia Records Project and the evolution of psychoanalytic outcome research. In T. Shapiro & R. N. Emde (Eds.), *Research in psychoanalysis: Process, development, outcome.* Madison, CT: International Universities Press, pp. 279–297.

Bachrach, H. M., Weber, J. J., & Solomon, M. (1985). Factors associated with the outcome of psychoanalysis (clinical and methodological considerations): Report of the Columbia Psychoanalytic Center Research Project (IV). *International Review of Psycho-Analysis, 12,* 379–388.

Berghout, C. C., & Zevalkink, J. (2009). Clinical significance of long-term psychoanalytic treatment. *Bulletin of the Menninger Clinic, 73,* 7–33.

Berghout, C. C., Zevalkink, J., & Hakkaart-van Roijen, L. (2010). A cost–utility analysis of psychoanalysis versus psychoanalytic psychotherapy. *International Journal of Technology Assessment in Health Care, 26,* 3–10.

Berghout, C. C., Zevalkink, J., Katzko, M. W., & deJong, J. T. (2012). Changes in symptoms and interpersonal problems during the first 2 years of long-term psychoanalytic psychotherapy and psychoanalysis. *Psychology and Psychotherapy: Theory, Research and Practice, 85,* 203–219.

Beutel, M., & Rasting, M. (2002). Long-term treatments from the perspectives of the former patients. In M. Leuzinger-Bohleber & M. Target (Eds.), *Outcomes of psychoanalytic treatment: Perspectives for therapists and researchers.* London: Whurr Publishers, pp. 130–142.

Blatt, S. J. (1992). The differential effect of psychotherapy and psychoanalysis on anaclitic and introjective patients: The Menninger Psychotherapy Research Project revisited. *Journal of the American Psychoanalytic Association, 40(3),* 691–724.

Blatt, S. J., & Shahar, G. (2004). Psychoanalysis: For what, with whom, and how: A comparison with psychotherapy. *Journal of the American Psychoanalytic Association, 52*, 393–447.

Blomberg, J., Lazar, A., & Sandell, R. (2001). Long-term outcome of long-term psychoanalytically oriented therapies: First findings of the Stockholm Outcome of Psychotherapy and Psychoanalysis Study. *Psychotherapy Research, 11*, 36–382.

Cheney, C. O., & Landis, C. (1935). A program for the determination of the therapeutic effectiveness of the psychoanalytic method. *American Journal of Psychiatry, 91*, 1161–1965.

Coriat, I. H. (1917). Some statistical results of the psychoanalytic treatment of the psychoneuroses. *Psychoanalytic Review, 4*, 209–216.

Erle, J. B. (1979). An approach to the study of analyzability and analysis: The course of forty consecutive cases selected for supervised analysis. *Psychoanalytic Quarterly, 48*, 198–228.

Erle, J. B., & Goldberg, D. A. (1984). Observations on assessment of analyzability by experienced analysts. *Journal of the American Psychoanalytic Association, 32*, 715–737.

Erle, J. B., & Goldberg, D. A. (2003). The course of 253 analyses from selection to outcome. *Journal of the American Psychoanalytic Association, 51*, 257–293.

Falkenstrom, F., Grant, J., Broberg, J., & Sandell, R. (2007). Self-analysis and post-termination improvement after psychoanalysis and long-term psychotherapy. *Journal of the American Psychoanalytic Association, 55*, 629–674.

Feldman, F. (1968). Results of psychoanalysis in clinic case assessments. *Journal of the American Psychoanalytic Association, 16*, 274–300.

Grande, T., Dilg, R., Jakobsen, T., Keller, W., Krawietz, B., Langer, M., Oberbracht, C., Stehle, S., Stennes, M., & Rudolf, G. (2006). Differential effects of two forms of psychoanalytic therapy: Results of the Heidelberg-Berlin study. *Psychotherapy Research, 16*, 470–485.

Grande, T., Dilg, R., Jakobsen, T., Keller, W., Krawietz, B., Langer, M., Oberbracht, C., Stehle, S., Stennes, M., & Rudolf, G. (2009). Structural change as a predictor of long-term follow-up outcome. *Psychotherapy Research, 19*, 344–357.

Hamburg, D. A., Bibring, G. L., Fisher, C., Stanton, A. H., Wallerstein, R. S., Weinstock, H. I. & Haggard, E. (1967). Report of ad hoc committe on central fact-gathering data of the American Psychoanalytic Association. *Journal of the American Psychoanalytic Association, 15*, 841–861.

Huber, D., Henrich, G., Gastner, J., & Klug, G. (2012). Must all have prizes: The Munich Psychotherapy Study. In R. A. Levy, S. Ablon, & H. Kachele (Eds.), *Psychodynamic psychotherapy research: Evidence-based practice and practice-based evidence*. Totowa, NJ: Humana Press, pp. 51–69.

Huber, D., Klug, G., & von Rad, M. (2002). The Munich psychotherapy study: A process–outcome comparison between psychoanalysis and psychodynamic psychotherapies. In M. Leuzinger-Bohleber & M. Target (Eds.), *Outcomes of psychoanalytic treatments: Perspectives for therapists and researchers*. New York: Whurr Publishers, pp. 223–233.

Kantrowitz, J. L. (1986). The role of the patient–analyst 'match' in the outcome of psychoanalysis. *Annual of Psychoanalysis, 14*, 273–297.

Kantrowitz, J. L., Katz, A. L., Greenman, D. A., Morris, H., Paolitto, F., Sashin, J., & Solomon, L. (1989). The patient–analyst match and the outcome of psychoanalysis: A pilot study. *Journal of the American Psychoanalytic Association, 37*, 893–919.

Kantrowitz, J. L., Katz, A. L., & Paolitto, F. (1990a). Followup of psychoanalysis five to ten years after termination: I. Stability of change. *Journal of the American Psychoanalytic Association, 38*, 471–496.

Kantrowitz, J. L., Katz, A. L., & Paolitto, F. (1990b). Followup of psychoanalysis five to ten years after termination: II. Development of the self-analytic function. *Journal of the American Psychoanalytic Association, 38*, 637–654.

Kantrowitz, J. L., Katz, A. L., & Paolitto, F. (1990c). Followup of psychoanalysis five to ten years after termination: III. The relation between the resolution of the transference and the patient–analyst match. *Journal of the American Psychoanalytic Association, 38*, 655–678.

Kantrowitz, J. L., Katz, A. L., Paolitto, F., Sashin, J., & Solomon, L. (1987a). Changes in the level and quality of object relations in psychoanalysis: Followup of a longitudinal study. *Journal of the American Psychoanalytic Association, 35*, 23–46.

Kantrowitz, J. L., Katz, A. L., Paolitto, F., Sashin, J., & Solomon, L. (1987b). The role of reality testing in psychoanalysis: Followup of 22 cases. *Journal of the American Psychoanalytic Association, 35*, 367–385.

Kantrowitz, J. L., Paolitto, F., Sashin, J., Solomon, L. & Katz, A. L. (1986). Affect availability, tolerance, complexity, and modulation in psychoanalysis: Followup of a longitudinal, prospective study. *Journal of the American Psychoanalytic Association, 34*, 525–555.

Kernberg, O., Burstein, E., Coyne, L., Applebaum, A., Horowitz, L., & Voth, H. (1972). Psychotherapy and psychoanalysis: Final report of the Menninger Foundation Psychotherapy Research Project. *Bulletin of the Menninger Clinic, 26*, 3–275.

Klug, G. H., Filipiak, G., & Huber, B. D. (2012). Trajectories and mediators of change in psychoanalytic, psychodynamic and cognitive behavioral therapy. *Journal of the American Psychoanalytic Association, 60*, 598–605.

Knekt, P., Laaksonen, M. A., Harkanen, T., Maljanen, T., Heinonen, E., Virtala, E., & Lindfors, O. (2012). The Helsinki Psychotherapy Study: Effectiveness, sufficiency, and suitability of short- and long-term psychotherapy. In R. A. Levey, S. Ablon, & H. Kachele (Eds.), *Psychodynamic psychotherapy research: Evidence-based practice and practice-based evidence*. New York: Springer.

Knekt, P., Lindfors, O., Laaksonen, M. A., Renlund, C., Haaramo, P., Harkanen, T., Virtala, E., and the Helsinki Psychotherapy Study Group. (2011). Quasi-experimental study on the effectiveness of psychoanalysis, long-term and short-term psychotherapy on psychiatric symptoms, work ability, and functional capacity during a 5-year follow-up. *Journal of Affective Disorders, 132*, 37–47.

Knight, R. P. (1941). Evaluation of the results of psychoanalytic therapy. *American Journal of Psychiatry, 98*, 434–446.

Kubie, L. S. (1952). Problems and techniques of psychoanalytic validation and progress. In E. Pumpian-Mindlin (Ed.), *Psychoanalysis as science. The Hixon lectures on the scientific status of psychoanalysis*. New York: Basic Books, pp. 46–124.

Kubie, L. S., & Brenner, A. F. (1949). The objective analysis of psychotherapy. *American Journal of Orthopsychiatry, 19(3)*, 463–491.

Lazar, A., Sandell, R., & Grant, J. (2006). Do psychoanalytic treatments have positive effects on health and health care utilization? Further findings of the Stockholm Outcome of Psychotherapy and Psychoanalysis Project (STOPPP). *Psychotherapy Research, 16*, 51–66.

Leuzinger-Bohleber, M., Stuhr, U., Ruger, B., & Beutel, M. (2003). How to study the 'quality of psychoanalytic treatments' and their long-term effects on patients' well-being: A representative, multi-perspective follow-up study. *International Journal of Psychoanalysis, 84*, 263–290.

Leuzinger-Bohleber, M., & Target, M. (2002). *Outcomes of psychoanalytic treatment: Perspectives for therapists and researchers*. New York: Whurr.

Luborsky, L. (1962). Clinicians' judgments of mental health: A proposed scale. *Archives of General Psychiatry, 7*, 407–417.

Miles, H. H. W., Barrabee, E. L., & Finesinger, J. E. (1951). Evaluation of psychotherapy with a follow-up study of 62 cases of anxiety neurosis. *Psychosomatic Medicine, 13*, 83–105.

OPD Task Force. (Ed.) (2001). *Operationalized psychodynamic diagnostics: Foundations and manual*. Seattle, WA: Hogrefe & Huber.

Parloff, M. B. (1987). Reanalysis: Terminable and interminable. Review of Robert S. Wallerstein, Forty-two lives in treatment: A study of psychoanalysis and psychotherapy. The report of the Psychotherapy Research Project of the Menninger Foundation, 1954–1982. New York: Guilford Press, 1986. In *Contemporary Psychology, 32,* 856–857.

Rapaport, D. (1968). Psychoanalysis as science. *The Bulletin of the Menninger Clinic, 32(1),* 1–20.

Ruger, B. (2002). Statistical design and representativeness of the DPV follow-up study. In M. Leuzinger-Bohleber & M. Target (Eds.), *Outcomes of psychoanalytic treatment: Perspectives for therapists and researchers.* London: Whurr Publishers, pp. 121–129.

Sandell, R., Blomberg, J., & Lazar, A. (1997). When reality doesn't fit the blueprint: Doing research on psychoanalysis and long-term psychotherapy in a public health service program. *Psychotherapy Research, 7,* 333–344.

Sandell, R., Blomberg, J., & Lazar, A. (2002). Time matters: On temporal interactions in long-term follow-up of long-term psychotherapies. *Psychotherapy Research, 12,* 39–58.

Sandell, R., Blomberg, J., Lazar, A., Carlsson, J., Broberg, J., & Schubert, J. (2000). Varieties of long-term outcome among patients in psychoanalysis and long-term psychotherapy. *International Journal of Psychoanalysis, 81,* 921–942.

Sandell, R., Carlsson, J., Schubert, J., Grant, J., Lazar, A., & Broberg, J. (2006). Therapists' therapies: The relation between therapists' therapy and patient change in long-term psychotherapy and psychoanalysis. *Psychotherapy Research, 26,* 306–316.

Sashin, J. I., Eldred, S. H., & Van Amerongen, S. T. (1975). A search for predictive factors in institute-supervised cases: A retrospective study of 183 cases from 1959–1966 at the Boston Psychoanalytic Society and Institute. *International Journal of Psychoanalysis, 56,* 343–359.

Stone, L. (1954). The widening scope of indications for psychoanalysis. *Journal of the American Psychoanalytic Association, 2,* 567–594.

Wallerstein, R. S. (1986). *Forty-two lives in treatment: A study of psychoanalysis and psychotherapy.* New York: Guilford Press.

Wallerstein, R. S. (1995). *The talking cures: The psychoanalyses and the psychotherapies.* New Haven: Yale University Press.

Weber, J. J., Bachrach, H. M., & Solomon, M. (1985a). Factors associated with the outcome of psychoanalysis: Report of the Columbia Psychoanalytic Center research project (II). *International Review of Psychoanalysis, 12,* 127–141.

Weber, J. J., Bachrach, H. M., & Solomon, M. (1985b). Factors associated with the outcome of psychoanalysis: Report of the Columbia Psychoanalytic Center research project (III). *International Review of Psychoanalysis, 12,* 251–262.

Weber, J. J., Solomon, M., & Bachrach, H. M. (1985). Characteristics of psychoanalytic clinic patients: Report of the Columbia Psychoanalytic Center research project (I). *International Review of Psychoanalysis, 12,* 13–26.

Chapter 3

This project

> . . . gradualness. About this most important condition of fruitful scientific work
> I never can speak without emotion. Gradualness, gradualness, and gradualness.
> From the very beginning of your work, school yourselves to severe gradualness
> in the accumulation of knowledge.
>
> (Pavlov, 1936)

Introduction

We followed with great interest the development of the Shedler–Westen
Assessment Procedure-200 (SWAP-200), described below (cf. Shedler &
Westen, 1998; Westen & Shedler, 1999a, 1999b). It seemed to us that this clinician report measure had tremendous potential for studying change during
psychoanalysis. Certainly psychoanalysts are highly trained in recognizing and
thinking about each person with whom they work clinically. Further, although
there is a range of views about whether or not participation in research by
patients interferes with the analytic process, the fact that the SWAP-200 is a clinician report measure would also mean that the potential issue of interference
with analysis could be set aside.

We knew that a longitudinal study of psychoanalysis would mean a long-term
project since the average length of analysis in the United States approaches 6 years
(Doidge et al., 2002). Before we could seriously consider beginning a study that
we knew would continue for many years, we wanted experience with the central
measure and we wanted to know that it was likely to be sensitive to change over
time in psychoanalysis. To begin to work with the SWAP-200, we carried out
a study of clinician reports of partner-violent men in psychodynamic therapy
(Porcerelli, Cogan, & Hibbard, 2004). We had worked on research and clinical
work with people in partner-violent relationships for several years. The results
of our first study with the SWAP-200 were in accord with our research and
clinical experience. We then carried out two preliminary cross-sectional studies
of psychoanalytic outcome. In the first study, we asked analysts to complete the
SWAP-200 to describe a patient either beginning or ending analysis. The results

showed significantly healthier scores at the end of analysis in seven of the ten Personality Disorder Scales and positive changes in the High Functioning and Global Assessment of Functioning (GAF) scores (Cogan & Porcerelli, 2005). In the second study, analysts completed the SWAP-200 to describe patients who had recently ended analysis either with or without maximum benefits or to describe an ideal prototype of a patient at the end of analysis (Cogan, 2007). The groups differed in personality disorder, trait scale, and adaptive functioning scores in ways that supported the idea that the SWAP-200 was a reasonable measure for a longitudinal study. In both studies, the SWAP-200 items that were most endorsed also provided meaningful information. With these preliminary studies completed, we set to work on the present study.

Methods

The analysts

We began by recruiting analysts. We sent e-mail posts to the listserve of the American Psychoanalytic Association inviting analysts beginning a psychoanalysis to consider participating in the project. With recruiting posts once a month for 6 months, 78 analysts responded and then began participation in the project. The analysts were not compensated for their participation beyond our thanks in an e-mail each time we received research materials from them.

Measures

Analyst questionnaires

With the first mailing to each analyst willing to participate in the project, we included a 30-item questionnaire with questions about the analyst, the patient, and the analysis and a copy of the SWAP-200 (described below). In each subsequent mailing, we included a 12-item questionnaire with questions about the patient and the analysis and a copy of the SWAP-200. Both questionnaires included a question about the current GAF score of the patient, one of our adaptive functioning measures.

THE SHEDLER–WESTEN ASSESSMENT PROCEDURE-200

The SWAP-200 (Shedler & Westen, 1998, 2004; Westen & Shedler, 1999a, 1990b) includes 200 statements that might describe a person. A clinician working with the person sorts the statements into sets that describe the person from very well to not at all. These sorts are scored on scales for ten personality disorders, 11 traits and two adaptive functioning dimensions.[1]

Development   The SWAP-200 was developed from a background of concerns about the limits of both self-report measures and structured interviews for identifying personality disorders (Shedler & Westen, 1998; Westen & Shedler, 1999a, 1999b, 2007; Westen, Shedler, & Bradley, 2006). In practice, clinicians report that they find it quite useful to ask patients about characteristics of clinical disorders such as depression and anxiety. On the other hand, clinicians report that they assess personality characteristics of patients by recognizing themes in their own interactions with patients and in what patients say as they talk of their interactions with others (Westen, 1997). Over a period of years, Westen and Shedler developed a set of 200 items clinicians might use to quantify their observations of a patient. The items were developed from diagnostic criteria, the literature, clinical observation, and pilot studies and were refined and selected over a period of 7 years based on the responses of clinicians describing index patients, hypothetical prototypical patients with specified personality disorders, or a videotape of clinical interviews of patients (cf. Westen & Shedler, 1999a, 1999b). Of great importance in making the measure relevant and useful to clinicians working from any orientation, each item is written in clear, jargon-free, and theory-neutral language. The items include positive characteristics (e.g., "Is capable of sustaining a meaningful love relationship characterized by genuine intimacy and caring") as well as items that concern psychopathological features (e.g., "Tends to be arrogant, haughty, or dismissive").

The clinician rates each item in terms of how well or poorly it applies to the patient on a scale ranging from 7 (very well) to 0 (do not apply or are irrelevant). The number of items to be put in each response category is fixed, following Q-sort methodology (Block, 1971, 1978, 2008; Shedler & Block, 1990), with a truncated form of a normal distribution. In the original version of the SWAP-200, which we used here, each item is printed on a small card and the clinician literally sorts the cards into the pre-determined number of items in each category. There will be, for instance, eight items that describe the patient very well (category 7) and 100 items than do not apply or are irrelevant to the patient (category 0). The measure is also available in an electronic form.[2] In a study of consumer preferences, clinicians ranked the SWAP-200 the most clinically useful of five dimensional systems for diagnosing personality pathology (Spitzer, First, Shedler, Westen, & Skodol, 2008).

Reliability   The reliability of scores of the SWAP-200 items has been studied and has ranged from 0.61 to 0.90 in a variety of studies (e.g., Layne, Porcerelli, & Shahar, 2006; Lingiardi, Gazillo, & Waldron, 2010; Marin-Avellan, McGauley, Campbell, & Fonagy, 2005; Porcerelli, Dauphin, Ablon, Leitman, & Bambery, 2007; Shedler & Westen, 1998; Westen & Muderrisoglu, 2003).

PERSONALITY DISORDER SCALES

The clinician ratings are correlated with prototype scale scores to yield scores for the ten personality disorders of DSM-IV (American Psychiatric Association, 1994). These include paranoid, schizoid, schizotypal, antisocial, borderline, histrionic, narcissistic, avoidant, dependent, and obsessive personality disorders.[3] Each scale score is transformed to a T-score (with, therefore, a mean of 50 and a standard deviation of 10). T-scores of 55–59 indicate personality disorder features, while T-scores of 60 and above indicate a personality disorder.

Reliability   In two studies in the development of the SWAP-200, the internal consistency of the Personality Disorder Scale scores was high, ranging from 0.90 to 0.97 when clinicians described prototypical profiles, 0.81 to 0.93 when clinicians described actual patients, and 0.61 when clinician-judges completed the SWAP after each watched the same interview (with a corrected reliability of 0.75 for the two judges: Shedler & Westen, 1998). The 2–4-month test–retest reliability of the Personality Disorder Scale scores ranged from 0.64 to 0.96, with a median of 0.85 (Blagov, Bi, Shedler, & Westen, 2012). The 6-month test–retest reliability of the Personality Disorder Scale scores was high for psychoanalysts describing patients beginning psychoanalysis (r = 0.82), compared with the reliability for randomly paired cases (r = 0.02; Cogan & Porcerelli, 2012).

Validity   The SWAP-200 descriptions of actual and hypothetical patients with particular personality disorders matched, while those with unrelated diagnoses did not match (Shedler & Westen, 1998; Westen & Shedler, 1999a). In other words, convergent and discriminant validity were both good. Several studies of differences between known groups had SWAP-200 Personality Disorder Scale scores that differed in the expected ways (Cogan, 2007; Cogan & Porcerelli, 2005, 2012; Gazzillo et al., 2014; Lehmann & Hilsenroth, 2011; Marin-Avellan et al., 2005; Porcerelli, Cogan, & Hibbard, 2004). Several studies comparing Personality Disorder Scale scores and self-report measures of personality showed the expected relationships (Bradley, Hilsenroth, Guarnaccia, & Westen, 2007; Smith, Hilsenroth, & Bornsetein, 2009). Studies have found a relationship between Personality Disorder Scale scores and patient-rated treatment alliance scores (Smith, Hilsenroth, Fiori, & Bornstein, 2014) and between Personality Disorder Scale scores and associated countertransference reactions (Colli, Tanzilli, Dimaggio, & Lingiardi, 2014).

Several case studies have shown expected changes in Personality Disorder Scale scores over time with treatment (Gazzillo et al., 2014; Lingiardi et al., 2010; Lingiardi, Shedler, & Gazzillo, 2006; Porcerelli et al., 2007).

TRAIT SCALES

The SWAP-200 yields scores on 11 trait dimensions, derived from factor analysis of the 200 items.[4] These include psychopathy, hostility, narcissism, emotional dysregulation, dysphoria, schizoid orientation, obsessionality, thought disorder, oedipal conflict, dissociation, and sexual conflict. The clinician ratings are summed for items on each of the 11 Trait Scales.

Reliability One team of researchers has found a median inter-rater reliability of 0.82 for the trait scale scores (Westen & Muderrisoglu, 2006). Another team has found average 6-month test–retest reliabilities of 0.63 for the trait scale scores for matched cases and 0.05 for unmatched cases (Cogan & Porcerelli, 2012).

Validity Convergent validity of 0.66 and discriminant validity of −0.06 have been reported for the SWAP-200 Trait Scale scores of the treating clinician and scores based on videotapes of interviews of the patients (Westen & Muderrisoglu, 2006). Significant correlations between scores of the SWAP-200 and the NEO Personality Inventory – Revised (NEO-PI-R) have been reported for five of 11 scales (Mullins-Sweatt & Widiger, 2007).

ADAPTIVE FUNCTIONING SCALES

Finally, the SWAP-200 yields a score for Psychological Health, developed as a trait scale, and a score for an Insight scale, added as a trait scale (Lehmann & Hilsenroth, 2011). The clinician ratings are summed for items on each of the Adaptive Functioning Scales.

Reliability For the High Functioning Scale scores, one team has found an inter-rater reliability of 0.76 for two independent ratings of transcripts of four sessions at the beginning of therapy and 0.72 for ratings of transcripts at the end of therapy (Layne et al., 2006). For the High Functioning Scale scores, the 6-month test–retest reliability was 0.77 for matched cases and 0.00 for mismatched cases among people in psychoanalysis (Cogan & Porcerelli, 2012). For the Psychological Health Scale, the 6-month test–retest reliability was 0.79 for matched cases and 0.11 for mismatched cases among patients in psychoanalysis (Cogan & Porcerelli, 2012).

Validity The convergent validity of the Psychological Health Scale scores is high: $p = 0.79$ (Westen & Muderrisoglu, 2006). For the High Functioning Scale scores, known group differences have been in the expected direction (Cogan & Porcerelli, 2005, 2012, 2013; Porcerelli, Cogan, & Hibbard, 2004). In a case study of psychodynamic psychotherapy, adaptive functioning scores were higher at the end of treatment than at the beginning of treatment (Layne, Porcerelli, & Shahar, 2006).

Procedures

Seventy-eight analysts began participation in the longitudinal project. Of these, 12 (15.4%) stopped responding. Several of the analysts who stopped responding let us know that they had health or time problems; several did not respond to inquiries. Sixty analysts continued to report every 6 months until the index analysis ended. The rest of the analyses are still under way.

Outcome groups

There were five outcome groups. Patients in one group had a negative therapeutic reaction. The negative therapeutic reaction group is described in Chapter 4. There were two attrition groups. Patients in one attrition group dropped out of analysis and those in the second attrition group ended analysis because of external factors. The two attrition groups are described in Chapters 5 and 6 and are compared in Chapter 7. Patients in two groups completed analysis with mutual agreement between analyst and patient. Patients in one of these groups ended analysis with maximum benefits and those in the second group ended analysis without maximum benefits. These are described in Chapters 8 and 9 and are compared in Chapter 10.

Statistical analyses

For each of the outcome groups and comparisons, we carried out a sequence of statistical analyses first at the beginning and then at the end of the analyses. We begin by describing characteristics of the analysts, analyses, analysands, and SWAP items characteristic of the index group and those of other patients. Next, we compared characteristics of the relevant group with those of other patients statistically, following the same pattern described above. We compared demographic characteristics of the patients and of the analysts in the groups being compared using Wilcoxon two-sided comparisons with a t-approximation. Because there were multiple comparisons, we required a p value ≤ 0.005 for comparisons of the demographic characteristics of the patients and comparisons of the characteristics of the analysts in the two groups being compared. For comparison of characteristics of the analysis, we required $p \leq 0.02$. For comparisons of the personality disorder and trait scale scores in the two groups being compared, we required $p \leq 0.03$. For comparisons of the adaptive functioning scale scores, we required a $p \leq 0.05$. These required p values approach a Bonferroni correction (Mundfrom, Perrett, Schaffer, Piccone, & Roozenboom, 2006) to control for the inflation of apparently statistically significant results when there are quite a few statistical comparisons.

In each case, the statistical comparisons between the index group and others include a regression analysis in which the 200 SWAP items were entered into a stepwise regression equation to see which item or items best predicted group membership, using a Lasso selection (Tibshirani & Saunders, 2005). The item predictions are important because, if we can identify salient characteristics of people at the beginning of analysis to provide information about what may be ahead, it should be helpful for the analyst in working with his or her patient. Our use of regression analyses, particularly when entering the 200 SWAP items to differentiate between the index group and other patients, may be surprising for some readers. There has been "something of a revolution in data analysis in the past 10 or so years," noted Babyak (2004). We used stepwise regression analyses to identify SWAP items, SWAP-200 Personality Disorder Scores, SWAP Trait Scale Scores and scores on Adaptive Functioning Scales (SWAP High Functioning and Insight scale scores and GAF scores) that best differentiated between the index group and other patients at the beginning and at the end of analysis. In order to correct for chance occurrences of significant correlations, we required that the predictor variables to be entered must decrease in size – each was required to have a partial R^2 smaller than the previously entered predictor variable – and must have increased the model R^2 significantly ($p \leq 0.01$).

We will now describe characteristics of the analysts, analyses, and analysands as the analyses began.

At the beginning

Each of the analysts who volunteered for the longitudinal project was a member of the American Psychoanalytic Association. They analysts were from all over the United States, with somewhat more on the east and west areas of the United States and from the southwestern United States. Only the northwest was not represented in the study. Considering what the analytic situations were like as the analyses began will tell us something about what a group of analyses were like in the United States early in the twenty-first century. This look at 60 analysts, analysands, and analyses as the analyses began will also give us background for what is ahead. We can reflect on what the analyses were like as they began and can make some private guesses about what will predict analytic outcomes. Will the analysts' professional identity, the amount of their professional or psychoanalytic experience, or perhaps their theoretical orientation be the best predictor of the analytic outcomes? Or perhaps the frequency of analytic meetings will matter most. On the other hand, perhaps characteristics of the analysands as the analyses began will prove to be the best predictors. For the moment, in this chapter we do not know the outcomes just as neither the analyst nor the analysand knows the outcome as the analysis begins.

A caveat is in order immediately. We have longitudinal data describing 60 completed analyses. In some instances, analysts who described an index case at the beginning of analysis responded to the short questionnaire and completed the SWAP every 6 months for some time but eventually were willing to respond only to the questionnaire. Eleven cases were not complete with respect to the SWAP. Six additional analyses are still under way. Although the problems of incomplete data are characteristic of all research, these issues particularly need to be considered in longitudinal work because of the possibility of selective dropping out. We have compared the characteristics of analysts, patients, and the analytic situation of the cases that continued and the cases lost to follow-up. We have also compared completed cases with and without complete SWAP data. There were no differences between the groups that reached or even approached statistical significance.

In what follows, we will describe characteristics of the analysts, analysands, and analyses of the 60 cases for which we have complete data at the beginning of the analysis and at least a report of the outcome at the end of analysis.

The analysts

The analysts were diverse, as can be seen in Table 3.1. There were more women than men. Most were White – non-Hispanic. Almost half of the analysts were psychiatrists, but about a quarter were psychologists, about a quarter were social workers, and a few reported other professional orientations. The analysts had, on the average, more than 20 years of professional experience and more than 10 years of psychoanalytic experience, beginning with their first analytic case. Three analysts were describing their very first analytic case; three had more than 40 years of analytic experience. The theoretical orientations of the analysts varied. Almost half of the analysts were "theoretical purists" and more than half reported endorsing more than one theoretical orientation. Among the theoretical orientations, object relations, ego psychology, and drive/conflict theory were most represented, but self-psychology and other orientations were also endorsed.

Table 3.1 Characteristics of the analysts, analysands, and analyses

Characteristics of the analysts, analysands, and analyses	N (%) or mean (SD)
Characteristics of the analysts	
Sex	
Male	22 (36.7)
Female	38 (63.3)
Race	
Black/African American	2 (3.3)
Hispanic	2 (3.3)
White – non-Hispanic	56 (93.3)
Profession	
Psychiatrist	27 (45.0)
Psychologist	14 (23.0)
Social worker	16 (26.7)
Other	3 (5.0)
Professional experience (years)	21.0 (11.8)
Psychoanalytic experience (years)	10.5 (10.7)
Primary practice setting	
Private practice	57 (95.0)
Other	3 (5.0)
Primary theoretical orientation	
Drive/conflict	35 (58.3)
Ego psychology	38 (63.3)

Object relations	35 (58.3)
Self-psychology	10 (16.7)
Other	12 (20.0)
Number of theories endorsed	
One	27 (45.0)
Two	9 (15.0)
Three	15 (25.0)
Four	5 (8.3)
Five	4 (6.7)
Characteristics of the analysands	
Age	36.8 (10.4)
Sex	
Male	28 (46.7)
Female	32 (53.3)
Marital status	
Married	23 (38.3)
Committed relationship	9 (15.0)
Divorced	6 (10.0)
Single	2 (3.3)
Other	20 (33.3)
Race	
White – non-Hispanic	54 (90.0)
Other	6 (10.0)
Socioeconomic status	
Poor or working class	2 (3.3)
Middle class	23 (38.3)
Upper-middle class	27 (45.0)
Upper class	8 (13.3)
Education	
Some college	8 (13.3)
College	17 (28.3)
Graduate/professional	35 (58.3)
Alcohol use problems	
No	48 (80.0)
Unclear	9 (15.0)
Yes	3 (5.0)
Drug use problems	
No	53 (88.3)
Unclear	5 (8.3)
Yes	2 (3.3)

(continued)

Table 3.1 (continued)

Characteristics of the analysts, analysands, and analyses	N (%) or mean (SD)
Axis I clinical diagnosis	
None	6 (10.0)
Anxiety	18 (30.0)
Depression	19 (31.7)
Mixed	10 (16.6)
Other	3 (5.0)
Axis II clinical diagnosis	
None	15 (25.9)
Cluster A	
Paranoid	0 (0.0)
Schizoid	0 (0.0)
Schizotypal	1 (1.7)
Cluster B	
Antisocial	0 (0.0)
Borderline	2 (3.3)
Histrionic	6 (10.0)
Narcissistic	3 (5.0)
Cluster C	
Avoidant	5 (8.3)
Dependent	3 (5.0)
Obsessive	4 (6.7)
Personality disorder not otherwise specified	15 (25.0)
Psychiatric hospitalizations in the last 5 years	
No	59 (98.3)
Yes	1 (1.7)
Previous mental health treatment	
No	17 (28.3)
Once	30 (50.0)
More than once	13 (21.7)
Psychotropic medication	
None	30 (50.0)
One	20 (33.3)
Two	6 (10.0)
Three	4 (6.7)
Type of psychotropic medication	
Anti-depressant	27 (45.0)
Anti-anxiety	7 (11.7)
Anti-psychotic	2 (3.3)
Other	8 (13.3)

Characteristics of the analyses

Months of analysis at the first report Setting	1.7 (0.6)
Private practice	57 (95.0)
Other	3 (5.0)
Frequency	
Three times a week	12 (20.0)
Four times a week	43 (71.7)
Five times a week	5 (8.3)
Couch	
Yes	51 (85.0)
Generally	2 (3.0)
No	7 (11.7)
Fee	
Full fee	24 (40.0)
75% of full fee	13 (21.7)
50% of full fee	7 (11.7)
25% of full fee	10 (16.7)
Less than 25% of full fee	6 (10.0)

The analysands

The analysands were also a diverse group, as can be seen in Table 3.1. About half were men and about half were women. Most were White – non-Hispanic. Their marital status varied, although more than half were married or in a committed relationship. The analysts viewed more than half as having a socioeconomic status of at least upper-middle class. A very small percentage were of poor or working class. They were generally well educated and more than half had a graduate or professional education. Most had at least one Axis I clinical diagnosis, most often anxiety, depression, or mixed anxiety and depression. Many had at least one Axis II clinical diagnosis, most often Personality Disorder Not Otherwise Specified. Of those with a specific personality disorder, only one had Cluster A diagnoses. Only one had a psychiatric hospitalization in the last 5 years. On the other hand, almost three-quarters had previous mental health treatment. Half were taking psychotropic medication at the start of analysis.

The ten individual SWAP items that had the highest average rankings in the analysts' descriptions of the patients at the beginning of analysis are shown in Table 3.2. The analysts viewed the analysands as anxious, self-critical, guilty, and unhappy. On the positive side, the analysts also viewed the patients as having moral and ethical standards and responding to humor, and as being empathic, likeable, conscientious, and able to recognize alternative viewpoints.

Table 3.2 Shedler–Westen Assessment Procedure (SWAP) items that best describe
patients at the beginning of analysis

Item	Mean	SD
175. Tends to be conscientious and responsible	4.9	2.3
035. Tends to be anxious	4.8	2.3
120. Has moral and ethical standards and strives to live up to them	4.8	1.7
068. Appreciates and responds to humor.	4.7	1.9
091. Tends to be self-critical; sets unrealistically high standards for self and is intolerant of own human defects	4.7	2.2
057. Tends to feel guilty	4.4	2.5
059. Is empathic; is sensitive and responsive to other people's needs and feelings	4.4	2.0
051. Tends to elicit liking in others	4.3	1.9
111. Has the capacity to recognize alternative viewpoints, even in matters that stir up strong feelings	4.1	1.9
189. Tends to feel unhappy, depressed, or despondent	4.1	2.2

We consider three adaptive functioning scale scores. Psychological Health and Insight are Trait Scales from the SWAP. The GAF scale is a scale of adaptive functioning ranging from 1 (low) to 100 (high) in DSM-III and DSM-IV (American Psychiatric Association, 1980, 1994). The adaptive functioning scale scores show that, as the analyses began, the analysands were functioning reasonably well, as can be seen in Figure 3.1. The average SWAP Personality Disorder Scale scores were higher on the three Cluster C Personality Disorder Scales – Avoidant, Dependent, and Obsessive – than the on the other Personality Disorder Scales, also shown in Figure 3.1. The average SWAP Trait Scale scores were highest for the Sexual Conflicts scale.

The analyses

Most of the analyses were carried out in a private practice setting. Seventy percent of the analyses began at four times a week and, as the analyses began, most of the patients were using the psychoanalytic couch. Since fees vary regionally, the fees were described in terms of the percentage of the analyst's full fee rather than in dollar amounts. The fees varied from a full fee to less than 25% of the full fee. Characteristics of the analyses as they began are shown in Table 3.1.

Conclusions

The analysts who volunteered to participate in this project varied in terms of profession and included people early in training as well as very experienced

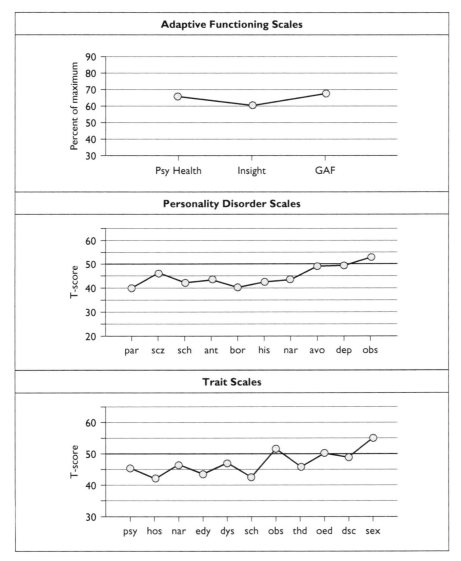

Figure 3.1 Adaptive functioning and Shedler–Westen Assessment Procedure (SWAP) scale scores at the beginning of analysis

Adaptive Functioning Scales: Psychological Health, Insight, Global Assessment of Functioning (GAF).

Personality Disorder Scales: Paranoid, Schizoid, Schizotypal, Antisocial, Borderline, Histrionic, Narcissistic, Avoidant, Dependent, and Obsessive.

Trait Scales: Psychopathy, Hostility, Narcissism, Emotional Dysregulation, Dysphoria, Schizoid Orientation, Obsessionality, Thought Disorder, Oedipal Conflict, Dissociation, and Sexual Conflict.

analysts. The analysts also varied in terms of their theoretical orientations. It will perhaps come as no real surprise to the reader to learn that the people who began analysis were generally well educated, many had been in some previous mental health treatment, and as a group they were functioning reasonably well in spite of experiencing anxiety and/or depression. It may be somewhat more surprising to learn that half were taking a psychotropic medication as the analyses began. The analyses were most often four times a week.

Twelve years have passed since the beginning of the project. Of the 60 analyses that have come to completion, a few ended with a negative therapeutic reaction, quite a few ended when the patient dropped out, and some ended because of reasons external to the treatment. Some ended with mutual agreement between analyst and analysand, in some cases without and in some cases with maximum benefits in the view of the analyst. We are now prepared to look at the situation at the beginning and end of analysis in each of these five ways that the analyses ended. Our hope is that we can learn about characteristics at the beginning of analysis that help predict how the analysis ended and that we can learn more about the characteristics of the patients at the varying endings of analysis.

Notes

1   Another dimension, called Q-factors, can also be scored. The Q-factors are not included here and we will not describe them. A revision of the SWAP-200, the SWAP-II, has also been developed (cf. Westen & Shedler, 2007).
2   Information is available at http://www.swapassessment.org/.
3   The Obsessive Personality Disorder is more like an introspective, high-level neurotic than DSM's rigid, rule-bound obsessive (Josephs, Anderson, Bernard, Fatzer, & Streich, 2004).
4   These scales are sometimes described as "factor T-scores" (e.g., Shedler, 2009).

References

American Psychiatric Association. (1980). *Diagnostic and statistical manual of mental disorders* (3rd ed.). Washington, DC: Author.

American Psychiatric Association. (1994). *Diagnostic and statistical manual of mental disorders* (4th ed.). Washington, DC: Author.

Babyak, M. A. (2004). What you see may not be what you get: A brief, nontechnical introduction to overfitting in regression-type models. *Psychosomatic Medicine, 66,* 411–421.

Blagov, P. S, Bi, W., Shedler, J., & Westen, D. (2012). The Shedler–Westen Assessment Procedure (SWAP): Evaluating psychometric questions about its reliability, validity, and impact of its fixed score distribution. *Assessment, 19,* 370–382.

Block, J. (1971). *Lives through time.* Berkeley, CA: Bancroft.

Block, J. (1978). *The Q-sort method in personality assessment and psychiatric research.* Palo Alto, CA: Consulting Psychologists Press.

Block, J. (2008). *The Q-sort in character appraisal: Encoding subjective impressions of persons quantitatively.* Washington, D.C.: American Psychological Association.

Bradley, R., Hilsenroth, M., Guarnaccia, C., & Westen, D. (2007). Relationship between clinician assessment and self-assessment of personality disorders using the SWAP-200 and PAI. *Psychological Assessment, 19(2),* 225–229.

Cogan, R. (2007). Therapeutic aims and outcomes of psychoanalysis. *Psychoanalytic Psychology, 24*, 193–207.

Cogan, R., & Porcerelli, J. H. (2005). Clinician reports of personality pathology of patients beginning and ending psychoanalysis. *Psychology and Psychotherapy: Theory, Research, and Practice, 78*, 235–248.

Cogan, R., & Porcerelli, J. H. (2012). Test–retest reliability and discriminant validity of the SWAP-200 in a psychoanalytic treatment sample. *Psychology and Psychotherapy: Theory, Research and Practice, 85*, 36–47.

Cogan, R., & Porcerelli, J. H. (2013). Validation of the Shedler–Westen Assessment Procedure Insight Scale. *The Journal of Nervous and Mental Disease, 201(8)*, 706–708.

Colli, A., Tanzilli, A., Dimaggio, G., & Lingiardi, V. (2014). Patient personality and therapist response: An empirical investigation. *American Journal of Psychiatry, 171(1)*, 102–108.

Doidge, N., Simon, B., Brauer, L., Grant, D. C., First, M., Brunshaw, J., Lancee, W. J., Stevens, A., Oldham, J. M., & Mosher, P. (2002). Psychoanalytic patients in the U. S., Canada, and Australia: I. DSM-III-R disorders, indications, previous treatment, medications, and length of treatment. *Journal of the American Psychoanalytic Association, 50*, 575–614.

Gazzillo, F., Waldron, S., Genova, F., Angeloni, F., Ristucci, C., & Lingiardi, V. (2014). An empirical investigation of analytic process: Contrasting a good and poor outcome case. *Psychotherapy (Chic), 51(2)*, 270–282.

Josephs, L., Anderson, E., Bernard, A., Fatzer, K., & Streich, J. (2004). Assessing progress in analysis interminable. *Journal of the American Psychoanalytic Association, 52(4)*, 1185–1214.

Layne, J. A., Porcerelli, J. H., & Shahar, G. (2006). Psychotherapy of self-criticism in a case of mixed anaclitic-introjective depression. *Clinical Case Studies, 5(5)*, 421–436.

Lehmann, M. E., & Hilsenroth, M. J. (2011). Evaluating psychological insight in a clinical sample using the Shedler–Westen Assessment Procedure. *The Journal of Nervous and Mental Disease, 199(5)*, 354–359.

Lingiardi, V., Gazillo, F., & Waldron, S. Jr. (2010). An empirically supported psychoanalysis: The case of Giovanna. *Psychoanalytic Psychology, 27(2)*, 190–218.

Lingiardi, V., Shedler, J., & Gazzillo, F. (2006). Assessing personality change in psychotherapy with the SWAP-200: A case study. *Journal of Personality Assessment, 86(1)*, 23–32.

Marin-Avellan, L. E., McGauley, G., Campbell, C., & Fonagy, P. (2005). Using the SWAP-200 in a personality-disordered forensic population: Is it valid, reliable and useful? *Criminal Behaviour and Mental Health, 15*, 28–45.

Mullins-Sweatt, S., & Widiger, T. A. (2007). The Shedler and Westen Assessment Procedure from the perspective of general personality structure. *Journal of Abnormal Psychology, 116(3)*, 618–623.

Mundfrom, D. J., Perrett, J. J., Schaffer, J., Piccone, A., & Roozenboom, M. (2006). Bonferroni adjustments in tests for regression coefficients. *Multiple Linear Regression Viewpoints, 32(1)*, 1–6.

Pavlov, I. (1936). Bequest of Pavlov to the academic youth of his country. *Science, 85(2155)*, 369.

Porcerelli, J. H., Cogan, R., & Hibbard, S. (2004). Personality characteristics of partner violent men: A Q-sort approach. *Journal of Personality Disorders, 18(2)*, 151–162.

Porcerelli, J. H., Dauphin, V. B., Ablon, J. S., Leitman, S., & Bambery, M. (2007). Psychoanalysis with avoidant personality disorder: A systematic case study. *Psychotherapy: Theory, Research, Practice, Training, 44(1)*, 1–13.

Shedler, J. (2009). *Guide to SWAP-200 Interpretation*. Unpublished manuscript. Aurora, CO: Department of Psychiatry, University of Colorado Denver School of Medicine.

Shedler, J., & Block, J. (1990). Adolescent drug use and psychological health: A longitudinal inquiry. *American Psychologist, 45,* 612–630.

Shedler, J., & Westen, D. (1998). Refining the measurement of Axis II: A Q-sort procedure for assessing personality pathology. *Assessment, 5(4),* 333–353.

Shedler, J., & Westen, D. (2004). Refining personality disorder diagnosis: Integrating science and practice. *American Journal of Psychiatry, 161(8),* 1350–1365.

Smith, S. W., Hilsenroth, M. J., & Bornstein, R. F. (2009). Convergent validity of the SWAP-200 Dependency Scales. *The Journal of Nervous and Mental Disease, 197(8),* 613–618.

Smith, S. W., Hilsenroth, M. J., Fiori, K. L., & Bornstein, R. F. (2014). Relationship between SWAP-200 patient personality characteristics and patient-rated alliance early in treatment. *The Journal of Nervous and Mental Disease, 202(5),* 372–378.

Spitzer, R. L., First, M. B., Shedler, J., Westen, D., & Skodol, A. E. (2008). Clinical utility of five dimensional systems for personality diagnosis: A "consumer preference" study. *The Journal of Nervous and Mental Disease, 196(5),* 356–374.

Tibshirani, R., & Saunders, M. (2005). Scarcity and smoothness via the fused lasso. *Journal of the Royal Statistical Society, 67,* 91–108.

Westen, D. (1997). Divergences between clinical and research methods for assessing personality disorders: Implications for research and the evolution of Axis II. *American Journal of Psychiatry, 154,* 895–903.

Westen, D., & Muderrisoglu, S. (2003). Assessing personality disorders using a systematic clinical interview: Evaluation of an alternative to structured interviews. *Journal of Personality Disorders, 17(4),* 351–369.

Westen, D., & Muderrisoglu, S. (2006). Clinical assessment of pathological personality traits. *American Journal of Psychiatry, 163,* 1285–1287.

Westen, D., & Shedler, J. (1999a). Revising and assessing Axis II, Part I: Developing a clinically and empirically valid assessment method. *American Journal of Psychiatry, 156(2),* 258–272.

Westen, D., & Shedler, J. (1999b). Revising and assessing Axis II, Part II: Toward an empirically based and clinically useful classification of personality disorders. *American Journal of Psychiatry, 156(2),* 273–285.

Westen, D., & Shedler, J. (2007). Personality diagnosis with the Shedler–Westen Assessment Procedure (SWAP): Integrating clinical and statistical measurement and prediction. *Journal of Abnormal Psychology, 116(4),* 810–822.

Westen, D., Shedler, J., & Bradley, R. (2006). A prototype approach to personality disorder diagnosis. *American Journal of Psychiatry, 163(5),* 846–856.

Part II

Comparing outcome groups

Chapter 4

Negative therapeutic reaction vs. others

> All happy families are alike but an unhappy family is unhappy after its own fashion.
> (Tolstoy, 1954/1978)

Introduction

While it certainly is not unusual for people to have a transient worsening of problems during psychoanalysis, occasionally more serious and persistent problems develop. Perhaps analysis did not or could not stop the development of a severe problem that was inexorably going to happen anyway. Or perhaps something about the analytic conversation created or exacerbated problems. These reactions are difficult for patients and for analysts.

When we consider the analyses in the longitudinal study that ended with a negative therapeutic reaction, we can, perhaps, begin to understand more about why these experiences are so difficult for patients, analysts, and researchers to talk about. Of the 60 analyses in the longitudinal study, 3 (5.0%) ended with a negative therapeutic reaction. One analysand became psychotic and was hospitalized. Two developed fixed and unyielding paranoid ideas about their analysts. Each of the analyses had continued for more than a year. Each of the analysts consulted with senior colleagues about the problems. In each case, the analyst hoped to continue working with the patient in psychotherapy rather than psychoanalysis.

Before we look closely at the three cases with a negative therapeutic reaction, we review the literature on the ideas about why negative outcomes occur in psychoanalysis and psychotherapy. Next we consider the empirical literature on the prevalence and predictors of negative outcomes in psychoanalysis and then in psychotherapy.

We are well aware that three cases is a modest number. Our hope is to learn something about how these negative therapeutic reactions might be anticipated and what they are like so that similar problems of others might be eased in the future.

Ideas about who has negative outcomes in psychoanalysis and psychotherapy

Psychoanalysis

Early in the development of psychoanalysis, Freud (1916/1981) wrote about someone "wrecked by success" and considered that guilt might be involved in the dynamics of this kind of paradoxical failure. This example is sometimes seen as Freud's first writing about the dynamics of the negative therapeutic reaction. He wrote of "negative reactions" in the "Wolf Man" case in 1918 (Freud, 1918/1981) and wrote in more detail about the problem in 1923, viewing the negative therapeutic reaction again as centered on guilt and the need for suffering. Here is Freud's description in *The ego and the id* (1923/1981):

> There are certain people who behave in a quite peculiar fashion during the work of analysis . . . Every partial solution that ought to result and in other people does result, in an improvement or temporary suspension of symptoms produces in them for the time being an exacerbation of their illness; they get worse instead of better. They exhibit what is known as a "negative therapeutic reaction" . . . we come to see that we are dealing with what may be called a "moral" factor, a sense of guilt.
>
> (p. 49)

Many of the subsequent theoretical and clinical considerations of people with negative therapeutic reactions in psychoanalysis have centered around *guilt* (Asch, 1976; Freud, 1922/1981; Gero, 1936; Lampl-de Groot, 1967; Langs, 1976; Levy, 1982; Loewald, 1972; Sandler, Dare, & Holder, 1973; Sandler, Holder, & Dare, 1970), *narcissism* (Abraham, 1919/1979; Asch, 1976; Gero, 1936; Horney, 1936; Klein, 1957/1975; Lewin, 1950, Limentani, 1972; McDougall, 1980; Olinick, 1964; Riviere, 1936; Rosenfeld, 1975), and *envy* (Abraham, 1919/1979; Horney, 1936; Kernberg, 1975; Klein, 1957/1975; Lane, 1985; Riviere, 1936; Rosenfeld, 1975).

Two recent books have focused on failures in analytic treatments (Goldberg, 2012; Reppen & Schulman, 2003). In neither of these thoughtful books are there suggestions about predicting negative therapeutic reactions. In a chapter in Reppen and Schulman (2003), Wallerstein notes that two of his early cases had a negative therapeutic reaction, perhaps of some comfort to others with this difficult experience, particularly early in their psychoanalytic training.

Psychotherapy

Negative therapeutic reactions occur in all types of psychotherapies (Loewald, 1972), as well as in psychoanalysis, although different approaches to treatment may conceptualize the reactions differently. Provoked by Eysenck's (1952, 1966) challenges about whether or not psychotherapy was effective at all – or perhaps whether only behavior therapy was effective (Eysenck, 1961) – and a resulting surge in empirical study of the outcomes of psychotherapy (cf. Smith, Glass, & Miller, 1980; Strupp, Hadley, & Gomes-Schwartz, 1977; Wampold, 2001), researchers noted the occasional occurrence of "deterioration effects" (Bergin, 1966, 1971; Bergin, Murray, Truax, & Shoben, 1963), "therapy-induced changes for the worse" (Mays & Franks, 1985), or "negative effects" (Strupp et al., 1977). The negative outcomes have been described as "a significant decline in one or more areas of a patient's functioning between the onset of psychotherapy and termination of therapy ... not restricted to those negative changes which are therapy induced" (Mays & Franks, 1985, p. 8). It is probably impossible to know either in general or in a particular case whether deterioration of someone in psychotherapy is therapy-induced or would have occurred similarly without therapy. It is also not clear how negative therapeutic reactions might best be measured. What is clear, however, is that, just as sometimes people in psychoanalysis have negative reactions that are not transient, sometimes people in psychotherapy have negative reactions.

Prevalence and predictors of outcomes with negative reactions in psychoanalysis and psychotherapy

Psychoanalysis

The psychoanalytic empirical literature on negative therapeutic outcomes is modest in scope.[1] Of 22 patients in analysis in the Menninger Hospital Project (cf. Wallerstein, 1986), of whom perhaps half would generally be considered to have been suitable for psychoanalysis, reviews of records showed that 6 (27%) had unmanageable transferences and were moved from psychoanalysis to psychotherapy. In a review of the records of the Columbia Psychoanalytic Center, 4% of 36 analyses ended with negative therapeutic reactions (Weber, Bachrach, & Solomon, 1985). Negative therapeutic outcomes were reported by the analysts of 2% of 126 patients in one study (Aronson & Weintraub, 1968) and 4–6% of 54 patients in another (Weber, Elinson, & Moss, 1965). Setting aside the Menninger data, perhaps 3–5% of patients in analysis have a negative therapeutic reaction. We found no empirical study focusing on predictors of negative therapeutic reactions in psychoanalysis.

Psychotherapy

The psychotherapy literature on negative outcomes is also modest in scope. Studies of psychodynamic therapy have found a negative therapeutic reaction in 2% of 210 patients (Rosenbaum, Friedlander, & Kaplan, 1956), 3–6% of 30 patients (Sloane, Staples, Cristol, Yorkston, & Whipple, 1975), 6% of 145 patients (Stone, 1985), 0% of 41 patients (Weber, Bachrach, & Solomon, 1985), and 4–6% of 732 patients (Weber et al., 1965). Perhaps, then, 3–6% of patients in psychodynamic therapy have a negative therapeutic reaction.

One study of behavior therapy found that 3% of 31 people had a negative therapeutic reaction (Sloane et al., 1975). Two studies of cognitive-behavioral therapy found 3–5% of 40 patients (Ogles, Lambert, & Sawyer, 1995) and 5% of 20 depressed patients (Mohr et al., 1990) had a negative therapeutic reaction. In a review of the literature, Gurman and Kniskern (1978) reported that 2.8% of 1,337 people in family therapy and 7.7% of 739 people in marital therapy had a negative therapeutic reaction. In gestalt therapy with depressed patients, 19% of 26 patients (Mohr et al., 1990) had a negative therapeutic reaction. Setting aside the last number, which is an outlier, perhaps approximately 5% of people in psychotherapies that are not psychodynamic have a negative therapeutic reaction. As was the case in studies of psychoanalytic outcome, we found no empirical studies focusing on predictors of negative therapeutic reactions in psychotherapy.

The present cases with and without a negative therapeutic reaction

We have two goals in considering the outcomes of psychoanalysis with a negative therapeutic reaction. First, learning about the characteristics of analyses early in analysis that predict the development of a negative therapeutic reaction should allow earlier recognition of the risks of this problematic outcome so that adjustments in treatment are possible. Second, learning more about exactly what patients who develop a negative therapeutic reaction are like should facilitate understanding of the problems. We compare the information about the analyses of three patients with a negative therapeutic reaction with information from the other analyses as the analyses began and as the analyses ended.

As the analyses began

Patients

Two of the three patients with a negative therapeutic reaction were women and one was a man. All three were White and single. Their average age was 29.0 years (SD = 7.8). One had a college education and two had a graduate or professional education. One was viewed as being middle class and two as being upper-middle class. All three had an Axis I clinical diagnosis, including two with anxiety and one with depression. Two had an Axis II clinical diagnosis, including one with Dependent Personality Disorder and one with Personality Disorder Not Otherwise Specified. One had possible alcohol problems and none had drug problems. None were taking psychotropic medication. One had been in treatment before. We explored differences in the characteristics of patients who developed a negative therapeutic reaction and others with a series of non-parametric analyses. No characteristics of the background or demographics of the patients significantly differentiated between the two groups. Wilcoxon p ranged from 0.04 to 1.00; as was described in Chapter 3, the adjusted p value we required for statistical significance of differences in the demographic characteristics of patients in the two groups was $p \leq 0.005$, which approached a Bonferroni correction.

In terms of the picture from individual SWAP items as the analyses began, patients in both groups were articulate, as can be seen in Table 4.1. Beyond this, though, the most characteristic SWAP items of patients who had a negative

Table 4.1 Shedler–Westen Assessment Procedure (SWAP) items at the beginning of analysis that best describe patients with a negative therapeutic reaction and others

Item	Mean	SD
Negative therapeutic reaction		
091. Tends to be self-critical; sets unrealistically high standards for self	6.7	0.6
033. Appears inhibited about pursuing goals or successes; aspirations or achievements tend to be below his/her potential	6.3	1.2
054. Tends to feel s/he is inadequate, inferior, or a failure	6.0	1.0
114. Tends to be critical of others	6.0	1.0
042. Tends to feel envious	5.7	2.3
084. Tends to be competitive with others (whether consciously or unconsciously)	5.7	1.5
092. Is articulate; can express self well in words	5.7	1.2
119. Tends to be inhibited or constricted; has difficulty allowing self to acknowledge or express wishes and impulses	5.7	1.2
174. Expects self to be "perfect" (e.g., in appearance, achievements, performance, etc.)	5.7	1.2
131. Has difficulty allowing self to experience strong pleasurable emotions (e.g., excitement, joy, pride)	5.3	0.6
Others		
092. Is articulate; can express self well in words	5.4	2.2
120. Has moral and ethical standards and strives to live up to them	4.9	1.8
175. Tends to be conscientious and responsible	4.9	2.3
035. Tends to be anxious	4.7	2.3
068. Appreciates and responds to humor	4.8	1.9
059. Is empathic; is sensitive and responsive to other people's needs and feelings	4.5	2.1
051. Tends to elicit liking in others	4.5	2.0
091. Tends to be self-critical; sets unrealistically high standards for self and is intolerant of own human defects	4.3	2.3
111. Has the capacity to recognize alternative viewpoints, even in matters that stir up strong feelings	4.1	2.0
057. Tends to feel guilty	4.3	2.3

therapeutic reaction make a bleak picture indeed. Among other characteristics, as the analyses began they were described as self-critical, inhibited about pursuing goals, feeling inadequate and, at the same time, critical and envious of others. The SWAP items that best described other patients included items describing them as anxious and unhappy but overall as warm and positive.

To consider patient factors at the beginning of analysis that best differentiated patients with a negative therapeutic reaction from others, we carried out a series of four stepwise multiple regression analyses considering SWAP items, Personality Disorder Scale scores, trait scale scores, and adaptive functioning scale scores. The SWAP items and scale scores that best differentiated between the two groups are shown in Table 4.2. At the beginning of analysis, the patients who developed a negative therapeutic reaction were characterized as more arrogant and as more lacking close friendships than others, while slightly *less* characterized than others in having a sense of self-importance, and slightly less characterized than others as lacking social skills: $R^2 = 0.59$. You

Table 4.2 Shedler–Westen Assessment Procedure (SWAP) items and scale scores early in analysis that differentiate between patients with a negative therapeutic reaction (NTR) and others

Item	NTR	Others	R	R²	F	p
	Mean (SD)	Mean (SD)				
Predictors of group membership						
SWAP items						
133. Tends to be arrogant, haughty or dismissive*	4.3 (2.5)	0.6 (1.4)	0.24	0.24	18.19	<0.0001
004. Has an exaggerated sense of self-importance	0.3 (0.6)	0.8 (1.4)	0.18	0.42	17.00	0.0001
160. Lacks close friendships and relationships*	3.7 (3.5)	1.0 (1.5)	0.09	0.51	10.57	0.002
193. Lacks social skills; tends to be socially awkward or inappropriate	0.0 (0.0)	1.0 (1.7)	0.08	0.59	10.36	0.002
Personality Disorder Scales						
Paranoid Personality Disorder	49.7 (8.0)	39.8 (6.4)	0.10	0.10	6.62	0.01
Trait Scales						
Schizoid	54.9 (4.9)	45.7 (7.6)	0.15	0.15	9.54	0.003
Adaptive Functioning Scales						
Insight	37.3 (22.1)	61.9 (11.8)	0.12	0.12	7.28	0.009

* These two items are the most useful predictors in the clinical situation, discussed in the text.

may notice that we are highlighting lacking close friendships rather than having a lower than usual sense of self-importance, which was the second item that entered the regression equation. We have done this for reasons having to do with clinical utility. The difference between patients who developed a negative therapeutic reaction (mean = 0.3, SD = 0.6) and other patients (mean = 0.8, SD = 1.4), although statistically significant, is too small to be practically useful. We will see in Chapter 5 that having an exaggerated sense of self-importance is greater, and will have clinical utility, among patients who drop out of analysis.

The SWAP Paranoid Personality Disorder Scale and SWAP Schizoid Trait Scale scores were higher for patients with a negative therapeutic reaction, and predicted group membership modestly – R^2 = 0.10 and R^2 = 0.15, respectively. On the Adaptive Functioning Scales, the SWAP Insight Scale scores were lower for patients with a negative therapeutic reaction (R^2 = 0.12). The scale scores are shown in Figure 4.1.

Analysts

Two of the analysts whose patients had a negative therapeutic reaction were women and one was a man. All three were White. One was a psychiatrist and two were social workers.

They had an average of 9.3 years of professional experience (SD = 6.7) and 2.7 years of psychoanalytic experience (SD = 2.3), in contrast to the analysts of other patients, who had an average of 21.6 years of professional experience (SD = 11.7) and 10.9 years of psychoanalytic experience (SD = 10.8), with Wilcoxon p < 0.03 and < 0.05 respectively. These differences in experience approached, but did not reach, the required adjusted statistical significance (p ≤ 0.005). Two analysts practiced in a clinic setting and one in a private practice setting. One endorsed three theories and two endorsed one theory as a primary theoretical orientation. Two said that ego psychology was a primary theoretical orientation and one each endosed drive theory, object relations theory, or "other" as a primary theoretical orientation. There were no statistically significant differences in the characteristics of the analysts in the two groups. Wilcoxon p ranged from 0.03 (years of professional experience) to 0.92.

Analyses

All three of the analyses with a negative therapeutic reaction were four times a week, on the couch. One was carried out in a private practice setting and two were in a clinic setting. One patient paid 75% of a full fee, one paid 25% of the full fee, and one paid less than 25% of the full fee. The average length of the analyses with a negative therapeutic reaction was 20.7 months (SD = 8.3). There were no statistically significant differences in the characteristics of the analyses in the two groups. Wilcoxon p ranged from 0.04 (setting of the analysis) to 0.67.

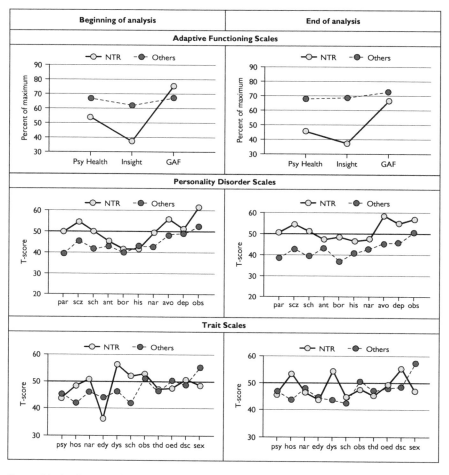

Figure 4.1 Analyses ending with a negative therapeutic reaction (NTR) and others at the beginning and end of analysis

Adaptive Functioning Scales: Psychological Health, Insight, Global Assessment of Functioning (GAF).

Personality Disorder Scales: Paranoid, Schizoid, Schizotypal, Antisocial, Borderline, Histrionic, Narcissistic, Avoidant, Dependent, and Obsessive.

Trait Scales: Psychopathy, Hostility, Narcissism, Emotional Dysregulation, Dysphoria, Schizoid Orientation, Obsessionality, Thought Disorder, Oedipal Conflict, Dissociation, and Sexual Conflict.

As the analyses ended

Patients

Forty-nine analysts provided SWAP data as well as questionnaire responses at the end of analyses that lasted for 6 months or more. The most descriptive SWAP items as the analyses ended are shown in Table 4.3. People in the two groups had *none* of the most descriptive SWAP items in common. As can be seen in Table 4.3, the items that best described people with a negative therapeutic reaction at the end of analysis were uniformly negative, in considerable contrast with the items that best described others at the end of analysis.

Stepwise regression analysis showed that three SWAP items best differentiated between the two groups at the end of analysis ($R^2 = 0.54$). At the end of analysis, patients whose analyses ended with a negative therapeutic reaction

Table 4.3 Shedler–Westen Assessment Procedure (SWAP) items at the end of analysis that best describe patients with a negative therapeutic reaction and others

Item	Mean	SD
Negative therapeutic reaction		
054. Tends to feel s/he is inadequate, inferior, or a failure	6.3	0.6
016. Tends to be angry or hostile (whether consciously or unconsciously)	6.0	0.0
025. Has difficulty acknowledging or expressing anger	6.0	1.0
114. Tends to be critical of others	6.0	1.0
084. Tends to be competitive with others (whether consciously or unconsciously)	5.3	2.9
042. Tends to feel envious	5.0	2.6
078. Tends to express aggression in passive and indirect ways (e.g., may make mistakes, procrastinate, forget, become sulky, etc.)	5.0	1.7
086. Tends to feel ashamed or embarrassed	5.0	2.0
163. Appears to want to "punish" self; creates situations that lead to unhappiness, or actively avoids opportunities for pleasure and gratification	5.0	1.7
167. Is simultaneously needy of, and rejecting toward, others (e.g., craves intimacy and caring, but tends to reject it when offered)	5.0	3.5
180. Has trouble making decisions; tends to be indecisive or to vacillate when faced with choices	5.0	1.7
Others		
092. Is articulate; can express self well in words	5.4	2.2
175. Tends to be conscientious and responsible	4.8	2.3
183. Is psychologically insightful; is able to understand self and others in subtle and sophisticated ways	4.8	2.2
068. Appreciates and responds to humor	4.7	2.2
120. Has moral and ethical standards and strives to live up to them	4.7	2.0
035. Tends to be anxious	4.5	2.1
111. Has the capacity to recognize alternative viewpoints, even in matters that stir up strong feelings	4.5	2.0
019. Enjoys challenges; takes pleasure in accomplishing things	4.3	2.4
59. Is empathic; is sensitive and responsive to other people's needs and feelings	4.3	2.4

were more likely to blame others for their problems, to feel that life has no meaning, and to have difficulty acknowledging or expressing anger, as can be seen in Table 4.4. The SWAP Psychological Health Scale scores of patients with a negative therapeutic reaction were lower than those of others ($R^2 = 0.34$). The SWAP Avoidant Personality Disorder Scale scores of patients with a negative therapeutic reaction were higher than the scores of other patients ($R^2 = 0.16$). No SWAP Trait Scale scores significantly differentiated between the two groups. The scale scores of patients in the two groups at the end of analysis are shown in Figure 4.1.

Table 4.4 Shedler–Westen Assessment Procedure (SWAP) items and scale scores at the end of analysis and length of analysis differentiate between patients with a negative therapeutic reaction (NTR) and others

Predictors of group membership	NTR Mean (SD)	Others Mean (SD)	r	R²	F	p
SWAP items						
014. Tends to blame others for own failures or shortcomings; tends to believe his/her problems are caused by external factors	4.0 (2.6)	0.9 (1.3)	0.24	0.24	14.9	0.0003
050. Tends to feel life has no meaning	2.7 (2.5)	0.6 (1.1)	0.17	0.41	13.23	0.001
025. Has difficulty acknowledging or expressing anger	6.0 (1.0)	3.1 (2.4)	0.13	0.54	13.02	0.001
114. Tends to be critical of others	6.0 (1.0)	2.7 (2.1)	0.08	0.62	9.41	0.004
021. Tends to be hostile toward members of the opposite sex, whetherconsciously or unconsciously (e.g., may be disparaging, competitive, etc.)	0.0 (0.0)	1.7 (1.9)	0.06	0.68	8.16	0.007
Personality Disorder Scales						
Avoidant	58.6 (1.9)	46.3 (7.2)	0.16	0.16	8.63	0.005
Trait Scales						
None are significant						
Adaptive Functioning Scales						
Psychological Health	45.7 (6.8)	67.5 (13.5)	0.34	0.34	7.57	0.009

Analyses

The analyses of the three patients with a negative therapeutic reaction and the 57 other patients did not differ in length (Wilcoxon $p = 0.50$).

Conclusions

In our longitudinal study, the prevalence of negative therapeutic reactions was much the same as reports of the prevalence in psychoanalysis and psychotherapy. We think that the longitudinal nature of the present data will prove helpful. We are, however, aware of a problem at this point that has to do with understanding what we can about characteristics at the beginning of analysis that suggest a risk of a negative therapeutic reaction. Rather than quietly throw a cloak of invisibility over the fact that averages are obscuring a problem, let us explore the situation. At the beginning of analysis, the patient who had a manic reaction in analysis had the highest possible score (a score of 7) on the SWAP item "Tends to be arrogant, haughty, or dismissive." No other patient in the study had a score of 7 on this item. At the beginning of analysis, the two patients who developed fixed negative transferences had moderate scores on the SWAP item "Tends to be arrogant"; both also had modestly elevated scores on the SWAP item, "Lacks close friendships and relationships." A stepwise regression analysis showed that these two items together differentiated these two patients from patients who did not have a negative therapeutic reaction ($R^2 = 0.51$).

We are particularly interested in the individual SWAP items at the beginning of analysis because they are the best predictors of what's ahead in the analysis and because they are easier to remember and notice than complex scale scores. Although these observations certainly need to be confirmed in other research, we suggest that an unusual degree of arrogance at the beginning of analysis is enough to provide a "red flag" of caution about what may be ahead in the analysis, particularly when it is combined with a lack of close friendships.

At the end of analysis too, the individual SWAP items differentiated between patients with and without a negative therapeutic reaction better than scale scores or characteristics of the analysis or analyst. The patients with a negative therapeutic reaction were described as blaming others, feeling that life has no meaning, having more difficulties expressing anger than others, being critical of others, having more difficulties expressing anger than others, and also as being less hostile to members of the opposite sex than others ($R^2 = 0.68$). We think that you will join us in finding these items a poignant description of patients with a negative therapeutic reaction.

Note

1 Several surveys of the outcomes of psychoanalysis did not separate negative therapeutic outcomes from dropping out of treatment (cf. Bachrach, Weber, & Solomon, 1985; Coriat, 1917; Feldman, 1968; Knight, 1941; Sashin, Eldred, & Van Amerongen, 1975).

References

Abraham, K. (1919). A particular form of neurotic resistance against the psycho-analytic method. In K. Abraham (Ed.), *Selected papers on psycho-analysis*. New York: Brunner/Mazel, pp. 303–311. (Reprinted in 1979.)

Aronson, H., & Weintraub, W. (1968). Social background of the patient in classical psychoanalysis. *The Journal of Nervous and Mental Disease, 146*, 91–97.

Asch, S. S. (1976). Varieties of negative therapeutic reaction and problems of technique. *Journal of the American Psychoanalytic Association, 24*, 373–407.

Bachrach, H. M., Weber, J. J., & Solomon, M. (1985). Factors associated with the outcome of psychoanalysis (clinical and methodological considerations): Report of the Columbia Psychoanalytic Center Research Project (IV). *International Review of Psycho-Analysis, 12*, 379–388.

Bergin, A. E. (1966). Some implications of psychotherapy research for therapeutic practice. *Journal of Abnormal Psychology, 71(4)*, 235–246.

Bergin, A. E. (1971). The evaluation of therapeutic outcomes. In A. E. Bergin & S. L. Garfields (Eds.), *The handbook of psychotherapy and behavior change: An empirical analysis*. New York: Wiley, pp. 217–270.

Bergin, A. E., Murray, E. J., Truax, C. B., & Shoben, E. J. (1963). The effects of psychotherapy: Negative results revisited. *Journal of Counseling Psychology, 10*, 244–250.

Coriat, I. H. (1917). Some statistical results of the psychoanalytic treatment of the psycho-neuroses. *Psychoanalytic Review, 4*, 209–216.

Eysenck, H. J. (1952). The effects of psychotherapy: An evaluation. *Journal of Consulting Psychology, 16*, 319–324.

Eysenck, H. J. (1961). The effects of psychotherapy. In H. J. Eysenck (Ed.), *Handbook of abnormal psychology*. New York: Basic Books, pp. 697–725.

Eysenck, H. J. (1966). *The effects of psychotherapy*. New York: International Science Press.

Feldman, F. (1968). Results of psychoanalysis in clinic case assessments. *Journal of the American Psychoanalytic Association, 16*, 274–300.

Freud, S. (1916). Some character-types met with in psychoanalytic work. In J. Stracey (Ed. and transl.), *The standard edition of the complete psychological works of Sigmund Freud* (Vol. 14). London: Hogarth Press, pp. 309–336. (Reprinted in 1981.)

Freud, S. (1918). From the history of an infantile neurosis. In J. Strachey (Ed. and transl.), *The standard edition of the complete psychological works of Sigmund Freud* (Vol. 17). London: Hogarth Press, pp. 7–122. (Reprinted in 1981.)

Freud, S. (1922). Psychoanalysis. In J. Stracey (Ed. and transl.), *The standard edition of the complete psychological works of Sigmund Freud* (Vol. 18). London: Hogarth Press, pp. 235–254. (Reprinted in 1981.)

Freud, S. (1923). The ego and the id. In J. Stracey (Ed. and transl.), *The standard edition of the complete psychological works of Sigmund Freud* (Vol. 19). London: Hogarth Press, pp. 3–66. (Reprinted in 1981.)

Gero, G. (1936). Construction of depression. *International Journal of Psycho-Analysis, 17*, 423–461.

Goldberg, A. (2012). *The analysis of failure: An investigation of failed cases in psychoanalysis and psychotherapy*. New York: Routledge.

Gurman, A. S., & Kniskern, D. P. (1978). Deterioration in marital and family therapy: empirical, clinical and conceptual issues. *Family Processes, 17*, 3–20.

Horney, K. (1936). The problem of the negative therapeutic reaction. *Psychoanalytic Quarterly, 1*, 29–44.

Kernberg, O. F. (1975). *Borderline conditions and pathological narcissism*. New York: Jason Aronson.

Klein, M. (1957). Envy and gratitude. In M. Kahn (Ed.), *The writings of Melanie Klein, Volume 3*. London: Hogarth Press, pp. 176–235. London: Hogarth Press. (Reprinted in 1975.)

Knight, R. P. (1941). Evaluation of the results of psychoanalytic therapy. *American Journal of Psychiatry, 98*, 434–446.

Lampl-de Groot, J. (1967). Obstacles standing in the way of psychoanalytic cure. *Psychoanalytic Study of the Child, 22*, 20–35.

Lane, R. C. (1985). The difficult patient, resistance, and the negative therapeutic reaction: A review of the literature. *Current Issues in Psychoanalytic Practice, 1(4)*, 83–106.

Langs, R. (1976). *The bipersonal field*. New York: Jason Aronson.

Levy, J. (1982). A particular kind of negative therapeutic reaction based on Freud's "borrowed guilt." *International Journal of Psychoanalysis, 63*, 361–368.

Lewin, B. D. (1950). *The psychoanalysis of elation*. New York: Norton.

Limentani, A. (1972). The assessment of analyzability: A major hazard in selection for psychoanalysis. *International Journal of Psycho-Analysis, 53*, 351–361.

Loewald, H. W. (1972). Freud's conception of the negative therapeutic reaction, with comments on instinct theory. *Journal of the American Psychoanalytic Association, 20*, 235–245.

Mays, D. T., & Franks, C. M. (Eds.) (1985). *Negative outcome in psychotherapy and what to do about it*. New York: Springer.

McDougall, J. (1980). *Plea for a measure of abnormality*. Madison, CN: International Universities Press.

Mohr, D. C., Beutler, L. E., Engle, D., Shoham-Salomon, V., Bergan, J., Kaszniak, A., & Yost, E. B. (1990). Identification of patients at risk for nonresponse and negative outcome in psychotherapy. *Journal of Consulting and Clinical Psychology, 58(5)*, 622–628.

Ogles, B. M., Lambert, M. J., & Sawyer, J. D. (1995). Clinical significance of the National Institute of Mental Health Treatment of Depression Collaborative Research Program data. *Journal of Consulting and Clinical Psychology, 63(2)*, 321–326.

Olinick, S. L. (1964). The negative therapeutic reaction. *International Journal of Psychoanalysis, 45*, 540–548.

Reppen, J., & Schulman, M. (2003). *Failures in psychoanalytic treatment*. Madison, CT: International Universities Press.

Riviere, J. (1936). A contribution to the analysis of the negative therapeutic reaction. *International Journal of Psychoanalysis, 17*, 304–320.

Rosenbaum, M., Friedlander, J., & Kaplan, S. M. (1956). Evaluation of results of psychotherapy. *Psychosomatic Medicine, 18*, 113–132.

Rosenfeld, H. A. (1975). Negative therapeutic reaction. In P. L. Giovacchini (Ed.), *Tactics and techniques in psychoanalytic therapy, Vol. 2: Countertransference*. New York: Aronson, pp. 217–228.

Sandler J., Dare, C., & Holder, A. (1973). *The patient and the analyst: The basis of the psychoanalytic process*. Madison, CT: International Universities Press.

Sandler, J., Holder, A., & Dare, C. (1970). Basic psychoanalytic concepts: VII. The negative therapeutic reaction. *British Journal of Psychiatry, 117*, 431–435.

Sashin, J. I., Eldred, S. H., & Van Amerongen, S. T. (1975). A search for predictive factors in institute-supervised cases: A retrospective study of 183 cases from 1959–1966 at the Boston Psychoanalytic Society and Institute. *International Journal of Psychoanalysis, 56*, 343–359.

Sloane, R. B., Staples, F. R., Cristol, A. H., Yorkston, N. J., & Whipple, K. (1975). *Psychoanalysis versus behavior therapy*. Cambridge, MA: Harvard University Press.

Smith, M. L., Glass, G.V., & Miller, T. I. (1980). *The benefits of psychotherapy*. Baltimore, MD: Johns Hopkins University Press.

Stone, L. (1985). Negative outcome in borderline states. In D.T. Mays & C. M. Franks (Eds.), *Negative outcomes in psychotherapy and what to do about it*. New York: Springer, pp. 145–170.

Strupp, H. H., Hadley, S.W., & Gomes-Schwartz, B. (1977). *Psychotherapy for better or worse: The problem of negative effects*. New York: Jason Aronson.

Tolstoy, L. (1954). *Anna Karenina*. (R. Edmonds, transl.) New York: Penguin, p. 13. (Translation reprinted in 1978.)

Wallerstein, R. S. (1986). *Forty-two lives in treatment: A study of psychoanalysis and psychotherapy*. New York: Guilford Press.

Wallerstein, R. S. (2003). Reconsidering an analytic outcome: Success or failure? In J. Reppen & M. A. Schulman (Eds.), *Failures in psychoanalytic treatment*. Madison, CT: International Universities Press, pp. 121–152.

Wampold, B. E. (2001). *The great psychotherapy debate: Models, methods, and findings*. Mahwah, NJ: Lawrence Erlbaum.

Weber, J. J., Bachrach, H. M., & Solomon, M. (1985). Factors associated with the outcome of psychoanalysis: Report of the Columbia Psychoanalytic Center research project (III). *International Review of Psychoanalysis, 12*, 251–262.

Weber, J. J., Elinson, J., & Moss, L. M. (1965). The application of ego strength scales of psychoanalytic clinic records. In G. S. Goldman & D. Shapiro (Eds.), *Development in psychoanalysis at Columbia University: Proceedings of the 20th anniversary conference*. New York: Columbia Psychoanalytic Clinic for Training and Research.

Chapter 5

Attrition

Dropping out vs. others

> The treatment was not carried through to its appointed end, but was broken off
> at the patient's own wish when it reached a certain point.
>
> (Freud, 1905)

Introduction

Dropping out of treatments of all sorts is common. Although defining dropouts
can have complexities, the therapist's judgment of who has dropped out is face-
valid and is probably the best way to identify dropouts (Wierzbicki & Pekarik,
1993). In spite of a "relatively vast sea of literature" (Baekeland & Lundwall,
1975, p. 739), our ability to predict dropping out is quite limited. Of the 60
analyses in the longitudinal study, 23 (38.3%) were identified by the analyst as
having ended when the patient dropped out. Of these, six dropped out in the
first 6 months and six dropped out after having been in analysis for more than
3 years. Differentiating between early and late dropouts as well as differentiating
between patients who did and did not drop out may add to our understanding.

We found little in the way of ideas or theory about dropping out of psychoanalysis or psychotherapy and we begin by considering the empirical literature
on the prevalence and predictors of dropping out of psychoanalysis and psychotherapy. We then consider the analyses in this project as the analyses began
to learn what characteristics might predict a greater risk of dropping out. We
also consider differences between analyses that ended early and late in analysis.
Finally, we consider characteristics at the end of analysis to provide a clearer
picture of what patients are like when they drop out.

Prevalence and predictors of dropouts from psychoanalysis and psychotherapy

Psychoanalysis

The literature on dropouts from psychoanalysis is modest in scope. In a summary
of six early reports of psychoanalytic outcome, of 952 analyses 31% were "broken off" in the first 6 months (Knight, 1941). Of 2,983 analyses by members of

the American Psychoanalytic Association, 43% ended when the patient dropped out (Hamburg et al., 1967). Dropping out was less frequent for patients with psychosomatic problems and patients who were psychiatrists or psychoanalytic candidates and more frequent for patients with signs of schizophrenia. Of 126 patients in analysis in private practice, 20% dropped out (Aronson & Weintraub, 1969). Once again, patients with psychosomatic symptoms dropped out less often than others and patients who distorted reality dropped out more often than others. Of 130 highly screened patients in analysis with analytic candidates – only 6% of prospective analysands were accepted for treatment – at the Boston Psychoanalytic Institute, only 11.5% dropped out (Sashin, Eldred, & van Amerongen, 1975). Of 76 analyses of carefully screened patients in analysis with psychoanalytic candidates at the Columbia Psychoanalytic Center, 12% dropped out (Bachrach, Weber, & Solomon, 1985). Of 163 patients whose analysts were candidates at the Columbia Psychoanalytic Institute between 1995 and 2000, 29% dropped out (Cooper, Hamilton, Gangure, & Roose, 2004). Half of the dropouts were in the first 6 months of treatment. Dropouts were more often patients from the psychoanalytic clinic rather than patients who were originally from the candidate's private practice and were more likely to have an Axis II disorder in the borderline/histrionic/narcissistic spectrum than other patients. Of 116 analyses by graduates of the New York Psychoanalytic Institute Treatment Center between 1967 and 2000, 27% dropped out and of 92 analyses which began between 1984 and 1989, 36% dropped out (Erle & Goldberg, 2003). In two samples from the Columbia Clinic, 40% and 42% of training cases dropped out in the first year of analysis (Hamilton, Baldachin, & Roose, 2013; Hamilton, Wininger, & Roose, 2009). Finally, of 40 highly selected patients in psychoanalysis in Helsinki, Finland, and followed for 5 years, 5% dropped out because they were disappointed with the treatment (Knekt et al., 2011).

Perhaps the most consistent finding is that dropping out of psychoanalysis is frequent, with, generally, 20–40% of patients who begin analysis dropping out (Aronson & Weintraub, 1969; Bachrach et al., 1985; Erle & Goldberg, 2003; Hamburg et al., 1967; Knekt et al., 2011; Knight, 1941; Sashin et al., 1975). Very careful screening may be related to lower dropout rates (mentioned in Bachrach et al., 1985; Knekt et al., 2011; Sashin et al., 1975). We found no data on the prediction of dropouts from psychoanalysis. Our study seems to be the first study of its kind to consider personality features of patients as predictors of dropping out of psychoanalysis.

Psychotherapy

The most consistent finding in reviews of the literature on psychotherapy dropouts is that dropping out of psychotherapy is frequent, with 30–65% of people who begin psychotherapy dropping out (Baekeland & Lundwall, 1975; Barratt, Chua, Crits-Christoph, Gibbons, & Thompson, 2008; Brandt, 1965; Eiduson, 1968; Garfield, 1994; Hamilton, Moore, Crane, & Payne, 2011; Phillips, Wennberg, & Werbart, 2007; Rogers, 1951; Roos & Werbart, 2013; Sharf,

Primavera, & Diener, 2010; Wierzbicki & Pekarik, 1993). In a more recent review of the literature (Swift & Greenberg, 2012), the average weighted drop-out rate was 20%, far lower than in earlier reviews, perhaps reflecting a focus on studies of time-limited psychotherapy.

Predicting dropouts in psychotherapy has been of very limited success.[1] The role of demographic variables has been considered in meta-analyses and there has been some consistency in finding that younger adults and people from minority ethnicity groups were somewhat more likely to drop out than others (Baekeland & Lundwall, 1975; Barrett et al., 2008; Garfield, 1994; Reis & Brown, 1999). However, in their meta-analysis, Swift and Greenberg (2012, 2015) found that dropouts were younger and had less education than treatment completers. In studies where demographic variables could be coded continuously (e.g., per-cent minority ethnicity), dropout rates were higher for younger samples and samples with fewer women and fewer people in committed relationships.

Amid a great deal of inconsistency in findings, Baekeland and Lundwall (1975) found that social isolation was consistently related to dropping out of psychotherapy in 19 studies that considered this variable, and a lack of psycho-logical mindedness was related to dropping out in 24 of 26 relevant studies. Some years later, in a meta-analysis of 11 relevant studies, Sharf et al. (2010) found that dropping out was related to a weak therapeutic alliance; the effect size was moderate. On the other hand, in a large Canadian community health survey, the reason clients most often reported for ending psychotherapy was that they felt better (Westmacott & Hunsley, 2010). Both negative and positive fac-tors may be associated with dropping out of psychotherapy. Swift and Greenberg (2012) found that dropout rates were higher (29%) in treatments with no time limit and were higher (28.3%) in treatments that were not manualized. The team (Swift, Greenberg, Whipple, & Kominiak, 2012) considered that strategies that would foster the therapeutic alliance should help reduce premature termi-nation. Patients who dropped out of a cognitive-behavioral therapy without a pre-set time limit had lower levels of self-esteem and lower ratings of the thera-peutic alliance than other patients (Kegel & Fluckinger, 2014).

Dropouts and others in the present cases

As the analyses began

Patients

Of the 23 patients who dropped out, 12 were men and 11 were women. The average age of the patients was 39.0 years (SD = 9.6). Ten were married or in a committed relationship as the analyses began. Two had some college, nine had completed college, and 12 had a graduate or professional education. One was described as poor, ten as middle class, ten as upper-middle class, and two as upper class. Twenty had an Axis I clinical diagnosis at the beginning of analysis, most often anxiety ($N = 6$), depression ($N = 6$), or mixed anxiety and depres-sion ($N = 7$). Sixteen had an Axis II clinical diagnosis at the beginning of analysis, most often Personality Disorder Not Otherwise Specified ($N = 8$). As the analyses began, two patients had alcohol problems, two had possible alcohol problems, one had drug problems, and two had possible drug problems. Thirteen were taking psychotropic medication, most often antidepressant medication ($N = 12$). Eighteen had been in treatment before. We explored differences in the characteristics of patients who dropped out and others with a series of non-parametric analyses. No characteristics of the patients significantly differentiated between the two groups. Wilcoxon p ranged from 0.16 to 0.82.

In terms of the picture that can be drawn from individual Shedler–Westen Assessment Procedure (SWAP) items early in analysis, people in both groups were viewed as having many characteristics in common, as can be seen in Table 5.1.

Table 5.1 Shedler–Westen Assessment Procedure (SWAP) items at the beginning of analysis that best describe patients who dropped out and others

Item	Mean	SD
Dropouts		
092. Is articulate; can express self well in words	5.8	1.9
035. Tends to be anxious	5.0	2.1
068. Appreciates and responds to humor	5.0	1.6
086. Tends to feel ashamed or embarrassed	4.8	2.2
051. Tends to elicit liking in others	4.3	1.6
054. Tends to feel s/he is inadequate, inferior, or a failure	4.3	2.5
091. Tends to be self-critical; sets unrealistically high standards for self and is intolerant of own human defects	4.3	2.3
175. Tends to be conscientious and responsible	4.3	2.3
189. Tends to feel unhappy, depressed, or despondent	4.3	2.2
120. Has moral and ethical standards and strives to live up to them	4.2	1.6
149. Tends to feel like an outcast or outsider; feels as if s/he does not truly belong	4.2	2.0
Others		
175. Tends to be conscientious and responsible	5.3	2.2
120. Has moral and ethical standards and strives to live up to them	5.2	1.7
092. Is articulate; can express self well in words	5.2	2.1
091. Tends to be self-critical; sets unrealistically high standards for self and is intolerant of own human defects	4.9	2.1
035. Tends to be anxious	4.7	2.4
057. Tends to feel guilty	4.7	2.3
019. Enjoys challenges; takes pleasure in accomplishing things	4.6	2.0
068. Appreciates and responds to humor	4.6	2.1
059. Is empathic; is sensitive and responsive to other people's needs and feelings	4.5	2.2
025. Has difficulty acknowledging or expressing anger	4.4	2.0

Patients who dropped out, though, were characterized as tending to feel ashamed, like a failure, unhappy, and like an outsider, while other patients were seen as experiencing guilt, enjoying challenges, and having difficulty expressing anger.

We carried out a series of four stepwise multiple regression analyses to learn what characteristics at the beginning of analysis differentiated between the patients who dropped out and other patients, considering SWAP items, Personality Disorder Scales, Trait Scales, and adaptive functioning scores. A multiple regression analysis allows us to analyze multiple variables at the same time to learn which variables are most associated with the outcome of interest. The SWAP items at the beginning of analysis that best predicted dropouts are shown in Table 5.2. At the beginning of analysis, the patients who dropped out were

Table 5.2 Characteristics at the beginning of analysis that differentiate between patients who dropped out and others

Predictors of group membership	Dropouts Mean (SD)	Others Mean (SD)	r	R²	F	p
Patients who dropped out						
SWAP items						
149. Tends to feel like an outcast or outsider; feels as if s/he does not truly belong	4.2 (2.0)	2.3 (2.0)	0.18	0.18	12.14	0.001
S004. Has an exaggerated sense of self-importance	1.3 (1.9)	0.4 (0.7)	0.12	0.29	9.36	0.003
Personality Disorder Scales						
None are significant						
Trait Scales						
None are significant						
Adaptive Functioning Scales						
None are significant						
Patients who dropped out early	**Early M (SD)**	**Others M (SD)**				
SWAP items						
026. Tends to get drawn into or remain in relationships in which s/he is emotionally or physically abused	4.0 (3.0)	1.2 (1.8)	0.17	0.17	11.83	0.001

(continued)

Table 5.2 (continued)

Predictors of group membership	Dropouts Mean (SD)	Others Mean (SD)	r	R^2	F	p
Personality Disorder Scales						
None are significant						
Trait Scales						
None are significant						
Adaptive Functioning Scales						
None are significant						

Patients who dropped out late	Late Mean (SD)	Others Mean (SD)				
SWAP items						
153. Interpersonal relationships tend to be unstable, chaotic, and rapidly changing	1.5 (1.5)	0.2 (0.6)	0.24	0.24	17.71	<0.0001
020. Tends to be deceitful; tends to lie or mislead	2.2 (3.1)	0.2 (1.0)	0.23	0.47	24.05	<0.0001
Personality Disorder Scales						
Obsessive	44.9 (4.2)	53.7 (7.3)	0.13	0.13	8.4	0.005
Trait Scales						
Psychopathy	49.7 (5.2)	44.9 (3.0)	0.18	0.18	11.9	0.001
Adaptive Functioning Scales						
None are significant						

SWAP, Shedler–Westen Assessment Procedure.

described as feeling like an outcast or outsider, and were viewed as having a somewhat exaggerated sense of self-importance ($R^2 = 0.29$). No scale scores differentiated between patients who dropped out and others, as can be seen in Table 5.2 and Figure 5.1.

Analysts

Of the 23 analysts whose patients dropped out, ten were men and 13 were women. Twelve were psychiatrists, six were psychologists, and five were social workers. They had an average of 21.3 years of professional experience (SD = 11.7) and 10.7 years of psychoanalytic experience (SD = 10.7). More than half (56.5%) endorsed more than one primary theoretical orientation with 15

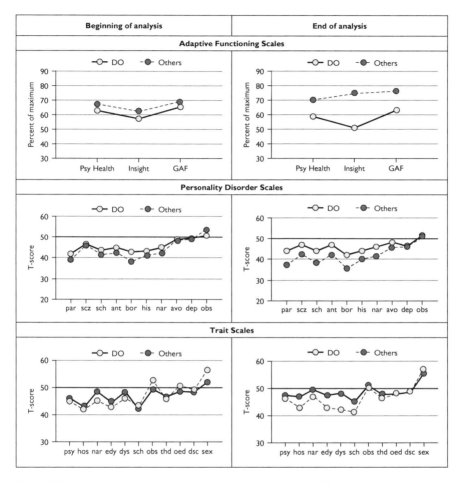

Figure 5.1 Analyses ending when the analysand dropped out (DO) and others at the beginning and end of analysis

Adaptive Functioning Scales: Psychological Health, Insight, Global Assessment of Functioning (GAF).

Personality Disorder Scales: Paranoid, Schizoid, Schizotypal, Antisocial, Borderline, Histrionic, Narcissistic, Avoidant, Dependent, and Obsessive.

Trait Scales: Psychopathy, Hostility, Narcissism, Emotional Dysregulation, Dysphoria, Schizoid Orientation, Obsessionality, Thought Disorder, Oedipal Conflict, Dissociation, and Sexual Conflict.

endorsing drive theory, 16 ego psychology, 11 object relations theory, five self-psychology and five endorsing other theoretical views. No characteristics of the analysts significantly differed between patients who dropped out and others. Wilcoxon *p* values ranged from 0.18 to 0.96.

Analyses

Of the 23 analyses that ended when the patient dropped out, six were three times a week, 14 were four times a week, and three were five times a week. All were in private practice settings and 20 were on the couch. The fees paid for analysis varied and included 11 patients who paid 100% of the analyst's full fee, two who paid 75% of the full fee, two who paid 50% of the full fee, five who paid 25% of the full fee, and three who paid less than 25% of the full fee. The average length of the analyses ending when the patient dropped out was 26.2 months (SD = 26.6). No characteristics of the analyses significantly differed between patients who dropped out and others. Wilcoxon *p* values ranged from 0.18 to 1.00.

Early vs. late dropouts

Patients

Of the 23 patients who dropped out, 6 dropped out in the first 6 months, 11 between 7 and 36 months, and 6 between 36 and 105 months of analysis. Stepwise regression analysis identified one SWAP item at the beginning of analysis that differentiated between patients who dropped out early in analysis and other patients and two items that differentiated between patients who dropped out late in analysis and other patients, shown in Table 5.2. Patients who dropped out early had higher scores on an item that concerned being drawn into relationships where s/he is emotionally or physically abused ($R^2 = 0.17$). Patients who dropped out late had higher scores than others on items that concerned having chaotic interpersonal relationships and tending to lie or mislead ($R^2 = 0.47$). Patients who dropped out later also had lower scores than others on the Obsessiveness Personality Disorder Scale ($R^2 = 0.13$), and higher scores than others on the Psychopathy Trait scale ($R^2 = 0.18$).

As the analyses ended

Dropouts vs. others

PATIENTS

Forty-nine analysts provided SWAP data as well as questionnaire responses at the end of analyses that continued for 6 months or longer. Of these, 17 patients had dropped out and 32 patients had not. The SWAP items most descriptive of patients who dropped out of analysis and other patients are shown in Table 5.3. As the analyses ended, patients in both groups were seen as articulate, appreciating humor, and conscientious, with moral and ethical standards. Patients who dropped out, however, were seen as feeling anxious, inadequate, and unhappy, having feelings of failure and shame, and as being self-critical, inhibited about achieving goals, and conflicted about authority. Other patients at the end of analysis were seen as enjoying challenges, being insightful, able to recognize alternative viewpoints, empathic, and able to maintain close friendships.

Table 5.3 Shedler–Westen Assessment Procedure (SWAP) items at the end of analysis that best describe patients who dropped out and others

Item	Mean	SD
Dropouts		
035. Tends to be anxious	4.8	2.1
092. Is articulate; can express self well in words	4.7	2.0
054. Tends to feel s/he is inadequate, inferior, or a failure	4.2	2.5
086. Tends to feel ashamed or embarrassed	3.8	2.8
068. Appreciates and responds to humor	3.8	2.3
189. Tends to feel unhappy, depressed, or despondent	3.8	2.4
175. Tends to be conscientious and responsible	3.7	2.3
033. Appears inhibited about pursuing goals or successes; aspirations or achievements tend to be below his/her potential	3.6	2.7
091. Tends to be self-critical; sets unrealistically high standards for self and is intolerant of own human defects	3.6	2.7
120. Has moral and ethical standards and strives to live up to them	3.6	2.2
129. Tends to be conflicted about authority (e.g., may feel s/he must submit, rebel against, win over, defeat, etc.)	3.6	1.8
Others		
092. Is articulate; can express self well in words	5.5	2.4
175. Tends to be conscientious and responsible	5.1	2.2
068. Appreciates and responds to humor	5.2	2.1
019. Enjoys challenges; takes pleasure in accomplishing things	4.9	2.3
183. Is psychologically insightful; is able to understand self and others in subtle and sophisticated ways	5.2	2.2
120. Has moral and ethical standards and strives to live up to them	4.9	1.9
111. Has the capacity to recognize alternative viewpoints, even in matters that stir up strong feelings	4.9	1.8
059. Is empathic; is sensitive and responsive to other people's needs and feelings	4.8	2.3
200. Is able to form close and lasting friendships characterized by mutual support and sharing of experiences	4.9	2.1
059. Is empathic; is sensitive and responsive to other people's needs and feelings	4.6	2.1

At the end of analysis, one SWAP item best differentiated between patients who dropped out and other patients. Patients who dropped out were less able than others to form close and lasting friendships ($R^2 = 0.28$). As the analyses ended, patients who dropped out had lower Global Assessment of Functioning and Insight scores than patients who did not ($R^2 = 0.41$). These are show in Table 5.4 and Figure 5.1.

Table 5.4 Patient factors at the end of analyses that differentiate between patients who dropped out and others and patients who dropped out early or late and others

Predictors of group membership	Dropout Mean (SD)	Other Mean (SD)	r	R^2	F	p
Patients who dropped out and others						
SWAP items						
200. Is able to form close and lasting friendships characterized by mutual support and sharing of experiences	2.3 (1.8)	4.9 (2.1)	0.28	0.28	18.58	<0.0001
141. Is extremely identified with a social or political "cause" to a degree that seems excessive or fanatical	1.4 (2.2)	0.2 (0.6)	0.14	0.42	11.32	0.002
148. Has little psychological insight into own otives, behavior, etc.; is unable to consider alternate interpretations of his/her experiences	2.0 (1.6)	0.5 (1.1)	0.09	0.51	8.32	0.006
Personality Disorder Scales						
Paranoid Personality Disorder	44.2 (7.2)	37.4 (7.3)	0.16	0.16	9.36	0.004
Trait Scales						
None are significant						
Adaptive Functioning Scales						
GAF	63.5 (6.8)	76.7 (10.9)	0.29	0.29	19.61	<0.0001
Insight	51.0 (19.4)	74.9 (18.3)	0.11	0.41	8.66	0.005
Patients who dropped out early	**Early** M (SD)	**Others** M (SD)				
SWAP items at the end of analysis						
None are significant						
Patients who dropped out late	**Late** M (SD)	**Others** M (SD)				
SWAP items at the end of analysis						
058. Has little or no interest in having sexual experiences with another person	3.2 (2.8)	0.5 (0.9)	0.33	0.33	23.49	<0.0001

134.	Tends to act impulsively, without regard for consequences	2.7 (2.3)	0.7 (1.1)	0.15	0.48	13.03	0.0008
SWAP items 6 months before the end of analysis							
177.	Repeatedly convinces others of his/her commitment to change but then reverts to previous maladaptive behavior; tends to convince others that "this time is really different"	2.8 (2.6)	0.2 (0.8)	0.38	0.38	22.6	<0.0001
044.	Perception of reality can become *grossly* impaired under stress (e.g., may become delusional)	1.4 (1.9)	0.1 (0.3)	0.21	0.59	18.9	0.0001

SWAP, Shedler–Westen Assessment Procedure; GAF, Global Assessment of Functioning.

ANALYSES

The analyses of the 23 patients who dropped out were shorter than those of the other 37 patients: 26.2 months (SD = 26.6) vs. 40.5 months (SD = 27.4), Wilcoxon $p = 0.02$.

Late dropouts vs. others

Two SWAP items at the end of analysis differentiated between patients who dropped out after 3 or more years of analysis and others. At the end of analysis, patients who dropped out late were viewed as having less interest than others in sexual experiences with another person, and more tendency to act impulsively ($R^2 = 0.48$). These views of the analysts – particularly the view of the patient as tending more than others to act impulsively – may be a consequence rather than really being a predictor of the patients having dropped out after some years of analysis. The items that differentiated between the two groups 6 months before the end of analysis were quite different. Six months before the analyses ended, patients who dropped out late were viewed as repeatedly convincing others of their commitment to change and reverting back to maladaptive behavior and as tending to become delusional under stress more than other patients ($R^2 = 0.59$). These are shown in Table 5.4.

Conclusions

Twenty-three of the 60 analyses (38.3%) were "broken off" by the patients. This number is somewhat conservative since analysts did not begin to participate in this research until the index analysis had been under way for 1.7 months on the average. No doubt some analyses not included here ended with the patient dropping out in the first few weeks. However, this prevalence of dropouts is similar to other work considering dropping out of psychoanalysis and psychotherapy. Perhaps the reader will be as surprised as we were to discover the similarity in dropout rates in psychoanalysis and psychotherapy. Neither literature mentions the other form of treatment.

Our quest here is to identify clues early in analysis that can help predict what may be ahead and to learn more about what patients are like as the analyses end in various ways. In terms of dropouts, it seems to us helpful to recognize that dropping out can occur in the first months of analysis, in the next year or two, or after several years of analysis. Perhaps helpful, if not surprising, is that the thread that seems to run through dropping out is problematic relationships with others.

As the analyses began, patients who dropped out of analysis felt more like outcasts than other patients. Early dropouts were more likely to be involved in abusive relationships than other patients. Although we hope these findings may be helpful, the predictive power in both cases was modest: $R^2 = 0.18$ and $R^2 = 0.17$, respectively.

The findings about late dropouts were especially interesting. As the analyses began, patients who dropped out after 3 or more years of analysis had more chaotic interpersonal relationships than other patients and tended to be more deceitful than other patients ($R^2 = 0.47$). Patients who dropped out late in analysis had lower scores on obsessiveness ($R^2 = 0.13$), and higher scores on psychopathy ($R^2 = 0.18$), than others. Although the predictive power of the personality disorder and Trait Scales are both low, the findings are in accord with the individual SWAP items and may be useful. An R^2 of 0.47 for the predictive power of the two individual items is of a sizeable magnitude in behavioral research. The items certainly call into question the patients' overall level of relatedness. Clinically the experience of people dropping out of analysis unexpectedly after several years can be surprising. Perhaps attending to these features may alert clinicians to dropping out.

At the end of analysis, patients who dropped out were viewed as being less able to form lasting friendships than other patients. Six months before they dropped out, patients who dropped out after 3 or more years of analysis were viewed as convincing others they were committed to change but reverting to the previous behavior and as having more impaired perceptions of reality under stress than other patients. With an R^2 of 0.59, these items are very likely to be useful in analytic work.

The items that characterize patients who dropped out involve problematic relationships with others. When the patient early in analysis feels like an outcast, tends to get drawn into abusive relationships, or tends to have chaotic interpersonal relationships, it is not surprising that the intensity of the analytic relationship and conversation is likely to be especially challenging for the patient. It seems very likely that a heightened awareness to these characteristics – to these SWAP items – early in analysis may be helpful as the analyst or therapist can bring them into the conversation. Similarly, it seems likely that if a patient late in analysis is deceptive with others about being committed to change, he or she is very likely to be deceptive about being committed to change in the analysis. Bringing this into the analytic conversation may well be helpful in reducing dropouts.

Note

1 We are setting aside the Prochaska model (cf., Brogan, Prochaska, & Prochaska, 1999), which involves predicting dropouts from short-term treatment at university counseling centers based on the questionnaire responses of clients.

References

Aronson, H., & Weintraub, W. (1969). Certain initial variables as predictors of change with classical psychoanalysis. *Journal of Abnormal Psychology, 74,* 490–497.

Bachrach, H. M., Weber, J. J., & Solomon, M. (1985). Factors associated with the outcome of psychoanalysis (clinical and methodological considerations): Report of the Columbia Psychoanalytic Center Research Project (IV). *International Review of Psycho-Analysis, 12,* 379–388.

Baekeland, F., & Lundwall, L. (1975). Dropping out of treatment: A critical review. *Psychological Bulletin, 82(5),* 738–783.

Barratt, M. S., Chua, W.-J., Crits-Christoph, P., Gibbons, M. B., & Thompson, D. (2008). Early withdrawal from mental health treatment: Implications for psychotherapy practice. *Psychotherapy: Theory, Research, Practice, Training, 45(2),* 247–267.

Brandt, L. W. (1965). Studies of "dropout" patients in psychotherapy: A review of findings. *Psychotherapy: Theory, Research and Practice, 2(1),* 6–12.

Brogan, M. M., Prochaska, J. O., & Prochaska, J. M. (1999). Predicting termination and continuation status in psychotherapy using the transtheoretical model. *Psychotherapy: Theory, Research, Practice, Training, 36(2),* 105–113.

Cooper, E. M., Hamilton, M., Gangure, D., & Roose, S. P. (2004). Premature termination from psychoanalysis: An investigation of factors contributing to early endings. *Journal of the American Psychoanalytic Association, 52,* 1233–1234.

Eiduson, B. T. (1968). Retreat from help. *American Journal of Orthopsychiatry, 38(5),* 910–921.

Erle, J. B., & Goldberg, D. A. (2003). The course of 253 analyses from selection to outcome. *Journal of the American Psychoanalytic Association, 51,* 257–293.

Freud, S. (1905). Fragment of an analysis of a case of hysteria. Postscript. In J. Strachey (Ed. and transl.), *The standard edition of the complete psychological works of Sigmund Freud* (Vol. 7). London: Hogarth Press, pp. 1–122. (Reprinted in 1981.)

Garfield, S. L. (1994). Research on client variables in psychotherapy. In A. E. Bergin & S. L. Garfield (Eds.), *Handbook of psychotherapy and behavior change* (4th ed.). Oxford, England: Wiley, pp. 190–228.

Hamburg, D. A., Bibring, G. L., Fisher, C., Stanton, A. H., Wallerstein, R. S., Weinstock, H. I., & Haggard, E. (1967). Report of ad hoc committee on central fact-gathering data of the American Psychoanalytic Association. *Journal of the American Psychoanalytic Association, 15*, 841–861.

Hamilton, M., Baldachin, J., & Roose, S. P. (2013). Follow-up on the dropout rate of training cases: Who and when. *Journal of the American Psychoanalytic Association, 61(3)*, 569–573.

Hamilton, S., Moore, A. M., Crane, D. R., & Payne, S. H. (2011). Psychotherapy dropouts: Differences by modality, license, and DSM-IV diagnosis. *Journal of Marital and Family Therapy, 37(3)*, 333–343.

Hamilton, M., Wininger, L., & Roose, S. P. (2009). Dropout rate of training cases: Who and when. *Journal of the American Psychoanalytic Association, 57(3)*, 695–702.

Kegel, A. F., & Fluckinger, C. (2014). *Predicting psychotherapy dropouts: A multilevel approach.* Wiley Online Library. doi: 10.1002/cpp.1899.

Knekt, P., Lindfors, O., Laaksonen, M. A., Renlund, C., Haaramo, P., Harkanen, T., Virtala, E., and the Helsinki Psychotherapy Study Group. (2011). Quasi-experimental study on the effectiveness of psychoanalysis, long-term and short-term psychotherapy on psychiatric symptoms, work ability, and functional capacity during a 5-year follow-up. *Journal of Affective Disorders, 132*, 37–47.

Knight, R. P. (1941). Evaluation of the results of psychoanalytic therapy. *American Journal of Psychiatry, 98*, 434–446.

Phillips, B., Wennberg, P., & Werbart, A. (2007). Ideas of cure as a predictor of premature termination, early alliance and outcome in psychoanalytic psychotherapy. *Psychology and Psychotherapy: Theory, Research and Practice, 80*, 229–245.

Reis, B. F., & Brown, L. G. (1999). Reducing psychotherapy dropouts: Maximizing perspective convergence in the psychotherapy dyad. *Psychotherapy: Theory, Research, Practice, Training, 36*, 123–136.

Rogers, C. (1951). *Client-centered therapy.* Cambridge, MA: Riverside Press.

Roos, J., & Werbart, A. (2013). Therapist and relationship factors influencing dropout from individual psychotherapy: A literature review. *Psychotherapy Research, 23(4)*, 394–418.

Sashin, J. I., Eldred, S. H., & Van Amerongen, S. T. (1975). A search for predictive factors in institute-supervised cases: A retrospective study of 183 cases from 1959–1966 at the Boston Psychoanalytic Society and Institute. *International Journal of Psychoanalysis, 56*, 343–359.

Sharf, J., Primavera, L., & Diener, M. J. (2010). Dropout and therapeutic alliance: A meta-analysis of adult individual psychotherapy. *Psychotherapy Theory, Research, Practice, Training, 47(4)*, 637–645.

Swift, J. K., & Greenberg, R. P. (2012). Premature discontinuation in adult psychotherapy: A meta-analysis. *Journal of Counseling and Clinical Psychology, 80(4)*, 547–590.

Swift, J. K., & Greenberg, R. (2015). *What is premature termination, and why does it occur? Strategies for engaging clients and improving outcomes.* Washington, DC: American Psychological Association.

Swift, J. K., Greenberg, R. P., Whipple, J. L., & Kominiak, N. (2012). Practice recommendations for reducing premature termination in therapy. *Professional Psychology: Research and Practice, 43(4)*, 379–387.

Westmacott, R., & Hunsley, J. (2010). Reasons for terminating psychotherapy: A general population study. *Journal of Clinical Psychology, 66*, 965–977.

Wierzbicki, M., & Pekarik, G. (1993). A meta-analysis of psychotherapy dropout. *Professional Psychology: Research and Practice, 24(2)*, 190–195.

Chapter 6

Attrition
External events vs. others

> My sessions with the Professor were barely under way, before there were pre-
> liminary signs and symbols of the approaching ordeal.
>
> (H. D., 1956)

Introduction

One of Freud's later analysands was H. D., a writer and a poet who lived in England. H. D.'s analysis with Freud was time-limited from the beginning and she went to Vienna for what was planned as 16 weeks of a 6-day-a-week analysis in 1933. There was growing unrest in Vienna, with Nazi bombing of Jewish-owned business escalating between 1933 and 1938, and the analysis was interrupted a few days early by a bomb scare uncomfortably close to Freud's office. Even without the onset of a war, in any time and place, patients' situations change. Patients may move as they complete college or graduate school or experience a job change, for instance. Analysts too may move. A patient or an analyst may have an incapacitating physical illness or even die. Any of these factors external to the treatment process may interrupt treatment. We will, again, follow the analyst's perspective on whether attrition from analysis is best considered as ending because of external factors. Of the 60 analyses in the longitudinal study, 17 (28.3%) ended because of external factors. We do not know about the external events that led to the end of analysis in every case but we do know that three patients completed college and relocated. One patient became critically ill. We also know that one analyst died and three analysts relocated. In other words, we know something about the nature of the external factors in eight of the 17 analyses.

As with endings of analysis from negative therapeutic reactions and endings from dropping out, we begin by considering the empirical literature on the prevalence and predictors of attrition from external factors in psychoanalysis and psychotherapy. We then consider the analyses in this project to see what, if any, characteristics at the beginning of analysis predict attrition from external factors and to have a clearer picture of what patients are like when they leave analysis because of external factors. Although the interruption of H. D.'s analysis because of bombing in the streets may give us pause, perhaps the reader, like other people, has sometimes wondered whether endings from external factors are really better characterized as dropouts. If the analyses characterized as ending because of external events in the longitudinal study truly ended because of external factors, and are not dropouts in disguise, we might expect that there are no predictors that differentiate these analyses from others.

Prevalence of attrition from external factors in psychoanalysis and psychotherapy

Psychoanalysis

Although Frayn (1992) found that life circumstances were more problematic among 119 patients who terminated prematurely from psychoanalytic training cases in the first year of treatment, we found only three studies in which patient attrition from analysis was separated into dropouts vs. terminations for reasons external to the treatment. Of 130 supervised cases, Sashin, Eldred, and Van Amerongen (1975) reported that 15 patients dropped out (11.5%) and eight ended analysis because of external factors (6.1%). Of 40 cases, Erle (1979) reported that 15 dropped out (37.5%) and seven ended analysis because of external factors (17.5%). Finally, Knekt et al. (2011), studying the first 5 years of 39 analyses, reported that two patients dropped out (5%) and three ended analysis because of external factors (10%).

Psychotherapy

Although there have been a number of thorough and thoughtful reviews of dropping out of psychotherapy (cf., Baekeland & Lundwall, 1975; Barrett, Chua, Crits-Christoph, Gibbons, & Thompson, 2008; Brandt, 1965; Greenspan & Kulish, 1985; Hamilton, Moore, Crane, & Payne, 2011; Joyce, 2007; Roos, 2011; Roos & Werbart, 2013; Sharf, Primavera, & Diener, 2010; Swift & Greenberg, 2012; Westmacott & Hunsley, 2010; Wierzbicki & Pekarik, 1993), these reviews rarely mention attrition from external factors. Baekeland and Lundwall (1975) noted that others had mentioned financial hardship, responsibility for dependants, fear of loss of employment, and an inability to afford treatment as reasons for people dropping out of medical treatments. Although these are certainly plausible external events that could well lead to attrition from psychotherapy, all of the events are negative. Absent from this list are more neutral reasons (e.g., a mandatory work relocation) and positive reasons why people might end incomplete treatments (e.g., obtaining employment in academia or a post-doctoral fellowship following graduate school). Therapists also may have external events that lead them to interrupt treatments (e.g., health problems or a necessary family relocation). Clearly, more work is needed to better understand attrition from external events.

The present cases terminating because of external events

As the analyses began

Patients

Of the 17 patients whose analyses ended because of external events, seven were men and ten were women. The average age of the patients was 34.1 years ($SD = 10.1$). Twelve were White – non-Hispanic, one was Hispanic, and four were not White – non-Hispanic, Black, or Hispanic. Ten were married or in a committed relationship, four were single, and three were divorced, widowed, or other. Their socioeconomic backgrounds varied, with one described as working class, four as middle class, nine as upper-middle class, and three as upper class. Twelve had a graduate or professional education, one had a college education, and four were in college. Fifteen had one or more Axis I clinical diagnoses, including five with anxiety, five with depression, one with mixed anxiety and depression, and six with other diagnoses. Ten had one or more Axis II clinical diagnosis, including three with an Avoidant Personality Disorder, one each with a Dependent, Histrionic, Narcissistic, Obsessive, or Schizotypal Personality Disorder, and two with Personality Disorder Not Otherwise Specified. Seven of the 17 patients whose analyses ended because of external events were taking psychotropic medications; all seven were taking antidepressant medication and two also taking another psychotropic medication. As the analyses began, two had possible alcohol use problems and one had possible drug use problems. Ten had been in treatment before. Patients whose analyses ended because of external factors and other patients had similar demographic characteristics. Wilcoxon p values ranged from 0.24 to 0.98.

In terms of the picture that can be drawn from individual Shedler–Westen Assessment Procedure (SWAP) items, early in analysis people in both groups had much in common, as can be seen in Table 6.1. Six of the ten items most characteristic of the patients whose analyses ended because of external events and of the other patients are the same and describe patients beginning analysis as conscientious, articulate, able to use their talents effectively, and able to recognize alternative viewpoints, with moral standards and a sense of humor. The patients whose analyses ended because of external factors were seen as enjoying challenges, able to use their talents effectively, feeling guilty, and able to recognize alternative viewpoints. The other patients were seen as empathic, likeable, feeling ashamed and depressed.

We carried out four stepwise multiple regression analyses to learn what differentiated patients who dropped out for external reasons from other patients at the beginning of analysis: SWAP items, Personality Disorder Scale scores, Trait Scale scores, and adaptive functioning scores. None of the stepwise regression analyses yielded any items or scales that predicted differences between the two groups. The SWAP scale and adaptive functioning scores are shown in Figure 6.1.

Table 6.1 Shedler–Westen Assessment Procedure (SWAP) items at the beginning of
analysis that best describe patients whose analyses ended because of external
factors and others

Item	Mean	SD
External factors		
175. Tends to be conscientious and responsible	5.7	2.0
019. Enjoys challenges; takes pleasure in accomplishing things	5.1	2.4
092. Is articulate; can express self well in words	5.1	2.5
120. Has moral and ethical standards and strives to live up to them	5.1	2.0
068. Appreciates and responds to humor	4.9	1.8
002. Is able to use his/her talents, abilities, and energy effectively and productively	4.8	2.2
035. Tends to be anxious	4.8	2.5
057. Tends to feel guilty	4.8	2.5
111. Has the capacity to recognize alternative viewpoints, even in matters that stir up strong feelings	4.8	2.1
091. Tends to be self-critical; sets unrealistically high standards for self and is intolerant of own human defects	4.6	2.4
Others		
092. Is articulate; can express self well in words	5.6	1.8
035. Tends to be anxious	4.8	2.2
120. Has moral and ethical standards and strives to live up to them	4.8	1.6
068. Appreciates and responds to humor	4.7	2.0
091. Tends to be self-critical; sets unrealistically high standards for self and is intolerant of own human defects	4.7	2.2
175. Tends to be conscientious and responsible	4.7	2.3
051. Tends to elicit liking in others	4.3	2.0
059. Is empathic; is sensitive and responsive to other people's needs and feelings	4.3	2.0
086. Tends to feel ashamed or embarrassed	4.2	2.0
189. Tends to feel unhappy, depressed, or despondent	4.2	2.2

We explored differences in the characteristics of patients whose analyses
ended for reasons external to the treatment and others. The patients in the study
included six who were ethnic minorities: one was Black, one was Hispanic and
four were "other." The analyses of five of these six patients ended for reasons
external to the treatment. Significantly more patients whose analyses ended for
reasons external to the treatment were ethnic minority than patients whose
analyses ended for other reasons; Wilcoxon $p = 0.002$. No other characteristics
of the patients significantly differentiated between the two groups. Wilcoxon p
ranged from 0.29 to 0.92.

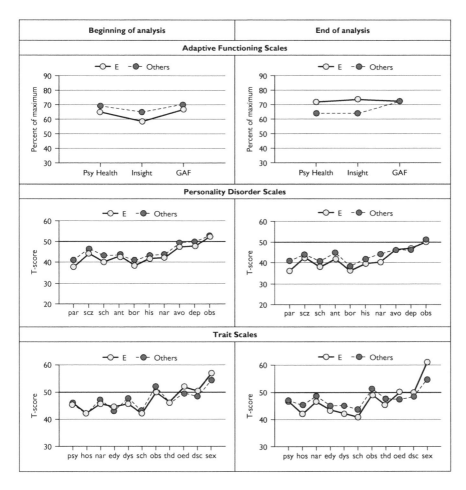

Figure 6.1 Analyses that ended because of external events (E) and others at the beginning and end of analysis

Adaptive Functioning Scales: Psychological Health, Insight, Global Assessment of Functioning (GAF).

Personality Disorder Scales: Paranoid, Schizoid, Schizotypal, Antisocial, Borderline, Histrionic, Narcissistic, Avoidant, Dependent, and Obsessive.

Trait Scales: Psychopathy, Hostility, Narcissism, Emotional Dysregulation, Dysphoria, Schizoid Orientation, Obsessionality, Thought Disorder, Oedipal Conflict, Dissociation, and Sexual Conflict.

Analysts

Of the 17 analysts whose patients' analyses ended for reasons external to the treatment, 12 were women and five were men. Sixteen were White/non-Hispanic and one was Black/African American. Six were psychiatrists, five were psychologists, five were social workers, and one was neither a psychiatrist, psychologist, nor social worker. Fourteen were in private practice and three were in other settings. They had an average of 21.8 years of professional experience (SD = 13.9) and 10.8 years of psychoanalytic experience (SD = 11.2). Drive theory was endorsed as a primary theoretical orientation by nine analysts, ego psychology by 11, object relations theory by nine, self-psychology by two, and other views by one. No characteristics of analysts of patients whose analyses ended because of external events and others differed significantly. Wilcoxon p ranged from 0.13 to 0.94.

Analyses

Of the 17 analyses, 12 were four times a week, three were three times a week, and two were five times a week. As the analyses began, 14 patients were on the couch and three were not. Fifteen were in a private practice setting and two were not. The fees paid varied and included eight patients who paid a full fee, four who paid 75% of a full fee, one who paid 50% of a full fee, two who paid 25% of a full fee, and two who paid less than 25% of a full fee. The average length of the analyses ending because of external events was 24.8 months (SD = 19.9).

No characteristics of the analyses differed between the two groups. Wilcoxon p ranged from 0.13 to 0.76.

As the analyses ended

Patients

Forty-nine analysts provided SWAP data as well as questionnaire responses at the end of analysis. The most descriptive SWAP items as the analyses ended are shown in Table 6.2.

Patients from both groups were seen as conscientious, appreciating humor, articulate, empathic, and enjoying challenges, with moral and ethical standards, and able to recognize alternative viewpoints. Patients whose analyses ended because of external events were seen as able to find satisfaction in the pursuit of long-term goals, empathic, and able to hear emotionally threatening information. Other patients tended to be competitive, able to use their talents productively, and able to form close and lasting friendships.

We carried out four stepwise multiple regression analyses to learn what differentiated patients who dropped out for external reasons from other patients at the end of analysis: SWAP items, Personality Disorder Scale scores, Trait scale scores, and adaptive functioning scores. None of the stepwise regression analyses yielded any items or scales that predicted differences between the two groups.

We have also considered changes in adaptive functioning scores from the beginning to the end of analysis with repeated measures analysis of variance

Table 6.2 Shedler–Westen Assessment Procedure (SWAP) items at the end of analysis that best describe patients who end analysis because of external events and others

Item	Mean	SD
External events		
175. Tends to be conscientious and responsible	5.7	2.0
092. Is articulate; can express self well in words	5.7	2.3
068. Appreciates and responds to humor	5.3	1.9
111. Has the capacity to recognize alternative viewpoints, even in matters that stir up strong feelings	5.3	1.0
196. Is able to find meaning and satisfaction in the pursuit of long-term goals and ambitions	5.3	1.8
059. Is empathic; is sensitive and responsive to other people's needs and feelings	5.1	1.9
183. Is psychologically insightful; is able to understand self and others in subtle and sophisticated ways	5.1	2.1
120. Has moral and ethical standards and strives to live up to them	5.0	2.1
019. Enjoys challenges; takes pleasure in accomplishing things	4.9	2.3
082. Is capable of hearing information that is emotionally threatening (i.e., that challenges cherished beliefs, perceptions, and self-perceptions) and can use and benefit from it	4.9	1.9
Others		
092. Is articulate; can express self well in words	5.0	2.3
035. Tends to be anxious	4.7	1.9
068. Appreciates and responds to humor	4.4	2.4
183. Is psychologically insightful; is able to understand self and others in subtle and sophisticated ways	4.3	2.4
120. Has moral and ethical standards and strives to live up to them	4.2	2.1
175. Tends to be conscientious and responsible	4.1	2.3
019. Enjoys challenges; takes pleasure in accomplishing things	3.9	2.5
084. Tends to be competitive with others (whether consciously or unconsciously)	3.8	2.4
111. Has the capacity to recognize alternative viewpoints, even in matters that stir up strong feelings	3.8	2.6
002. Is able to use his/her talents, abilities, and energy effectively and productively	3.7	2.3
200. Is able to form close and lasting friendships characterized by mutual support and sharing of experiences	3.7	2.4

tests comparing people whose analyses ended because of external factors and others. In terms of the three adaptive functioning scores, there was an increase in Global Assessment of Functioning scores from the beginning to the end of analysis ($F(1,42) = 5.71, p = 0.02$), and no differences in the change for people whose analyses ended because of external events and others ($F(1,42) = 0.12, p = 0.73$).

Analyses

The analyses of the 17 patients whose analyses ended because of external events did not differ in length from those of other patients: Wilcoxon $p = 0.11$.

Conclusions

At one level, we certainly do know that external events must interfere with ongoing treatments from time to time, particularly in treatments that often continue for some years. At another level, we may have had some index of suspicion about these endings. Finding no differences between patients whose analyses end for reasons external to the treatment and other patients, no differences between their analysts, and no differences in the characteristics of their analyses supports our recognition that in any long-term treatment reality factors can intrude. We think that these findings are helpful in understanding attrition in psychoanalysis. These data provide evidence that people truly do end analysis for reasons external to the treatment. This probably holds for psychotherapy as well. We are, of course, left with questions. Some questions will be left unanswered by our data. We wonder, for instance, about different types of external events that can interrupt an analysis. We began this chapter by noting the interruption of the analysis of H. D. by the escalation of bombs dropping not far from Freud's office. We noted that one of the analyses in the longitudinal study was interrupted when the analyst died. These situations are quite different from a patient accepting an offer for a job change and may be quite different from an analyst's moving from the area. Most immediately, with our data we are able to directly compare analyses characterized as ending when the patient dropped out and analyses characterized as ending because of external events. This we will do in the next chapter.

References

Baekeland, F., & Lundwall, L. (1975). Dropping out of treatment: A critical review. *Psychological Bulletin, 82(5),* 738–783.

Barratt, M. S., Chua, W.-J., Crits-Christoph, P., Gibbons, M. B., & Thompson, D. (2008). Early withdrawal from mental health treatment: Implications for psychotherapy practice. *Psychotherapy: Theory, Research, Practice, Training, 45(2),* 247–267.

Brandt, L. W. (1965). Studies of "dropout" patients in psychotherapy: A review of findings. *Psychotherapy: Theory, Research and Practice, 2(1),* 6–12.

Erle, J. B. (1979). An approach to the study of analyzability and analysis: The course of forty consecutive cases selected for supervised analysis. *Psychoanalytic Quarterly, 48*, 198–228.

Frayn, D. H. (1992). Assessment factors associated with premature psychotherapy termination. *American Journal of Psychotherapy, 56(2)*, 250–261.

Greenspan, M., & Kulish, N. M. (1985). Factors in premature termination of long-term psychotherapy. *Psychotherapy: Theory, Research, Practice, Training, 22(1)*, 75–82.

Hamilton, S., Moore, A. M., Crane, D. R., & Payne, S. H. (2011). Psychotherapy dropouts: Differences by modality, license, and DSM-IV diagnosis. *Journal of Marital and Family Therapy, 37(3)*, 333–343.

H. D. (1956). *Tribute to Freud with unpublished letters by Freud to the author.* New York: Pantheon. (pseud. Hilda Doolittle Aldington.)

Joyce, A. S. (2007). Patient-initiated termination. In A. S. Joyce, W. E. Piper, J. S. Ogrodniczuk, & R. H. Klein (Eds.), *Termination in psychotherapy: A psychodynamic model of process and outcomes.* Washington, DC: American Psychological Association, pp. 133–156.

Knekt, P., Lindfors, O., Laaksonen, M. A., Renlund, C., Haaramo, P., Harkanen, T., Virtala, E., and the Helsinki Psychotherapy Study Group. (2011). Quasi-experimental study on the effectiveness of psychoanalysis, long-term and short-term psychotherapy on psychiatric symptoms, work ability, and functional capacity during a 5-year follow-up. *Journal of Affective Disorders, 132*, 37–47.

Roos, J. (2011). *Left behind: A review of therapist and process variables influencing dropout from individual psychotherapy.* Sweden: Stockholm University, unpublished thesis.

Roos, J., & Werbart, A. (2013). Therapist and relationship factors influencing dropout from individual psychotherapy: A literature review. *Psychotherapy Research, 23(4)*, 394–418.

Sashin, J. I., Eldred, S. H., & Van Amerongen, S. T. (1975). A search for predictive factors in institute-supervised cases: A retrospective study of 183 cases from 1959–1966 at the Boston Psychoanalytic Society and Institute. *International Journal of Psychoanalysis, 56*, 343–359.

Sharf, J., Primavera, L., & Diener, M. J. (2010). Dropout and therapeutic alliance: A meta-analysis of adult individual psychotherapy. *Psychotherapy Theory, Research, Practice, Training, 47(4)*, 637–645.

Swift, J. K. & Greenberg, R. P. (2012). Premature discontinuation in adult psychotherapy: A meta-analysis. *Journal of Counseling and Clinical Psychology, 80(4)*, 547–590.

Westmacott, R., & Hunsley, J. (2010). Reasons for terminating psychotherapy: A general population study. *Journal of Clinical Psychology, 66*, 965–977.

Wierzbicki, M., & Pekarik, G. (1993). A meta-analysis of psychotherapy dropout. *Professional Psychology: Research and Practice, 24(2)*, 190–195.

Chapter 7

Attrition

Dropping out vs. external events

> The crumbs of knowledge offered in these pages . . . may serve as a starting-point for the work of other investigators, and common endeavor may bring the success which is perhaps beyond the reach of individual effort.
>
> (Freud, 1909/1981, p. 157)

Introduction

There is a puzzling dimension to the research literature, which tends to see attrition as a unidimensional issue. That is, dropping out and ending because of external events are not consistently differentiated in the research literature. Clinicians, however, see attrition from dropping out and attrition from external events as quite different events. Almost every psychoanalyst has had the experience of treating a young adult who begins treatment, for instance, when s/he begins graduate school or another type of professional training, successfully completes the professional training, finds employment in another locale, and leaves the analysis. Many analysts have had the experience of treating a young adult who completes an undergraduate program and moves to another area to go to on to graduate school or to begin other professional training. These endings are anticipated by analyst and analysands virtually from the beginning of the analysis and the anticipated endings will quite probably be talked about as part of the analytic work. Almost every clinician has had the experience of treating a professional who is promoted to a job that requires relocating and leaves the analysis. These changes are not very likely to have been anticipated since the analysis began but are likely to have been discussed in the analysis and so are not likely to be a surprise when they happen. If significant problems remain, a patient with a new job offer but no realistic need to move may be encouraged to stay until the analysis is complete. The situations of analysts too can change in ways that can interrupt treatment. Sometimes these can be anticipated and sometimes they cannot. These instances of attrition from external events are not rare and are surely viewed by both clinicians and patients as very different from the situation in which a patient simply drops out.

We did not find much literature that helped us understand experiences of dropping out from the perspective of the person in psychoanalysis or psychotherapy. People certainly can leave treatment because they feel better (cf. Westmacott & Hunsley, 2010), and this may include some people who drop out of psychoanalysis. However, it seems likely that when individuals drop out, they may be quite likely to have negative views of their treatment, of their experience of treatment, and perhaps of themselves as well. Abrupt dropping out is disquieting for the clinician as well as the patient. Dropping out is clearly frequent in psychoanalysis and psychotherapy and can be worrisome to all involved. Attrition from external events certainly can have complications as well for both analysands and analyst and we do not mean to minimize the difficulties of what are sometimes unexpected endings of analysis from external events. We certainly recognize that both types of attrition can present complications. Any information that will help us understand and deal with attrition when patients drop out and attrition because of external events may well be clinically useful.

Our comparisons of analyses ending when the patient drops out and other analyses in Chapter 5, and our comparisons of analyses ending because of external events and other analyses in Chapter 6 have supported the idea that the two attrition groups are different. In this chapter, we compare the two attrition groups directly to test our hypothesis that dropouts and patients whose analyses end because of external events really are two different groups. We also want see if we can make more finely tuned discriminations between the two attrition groups as they begin and as they end analysis. Differentiating between the two attrition situations may help us understand each group better and may be helpful in working with patients.

As the analyses began

Patients

As the analyses began, patients in both of the attrition groups were viewed as articulate and as responding to humor, with moral and ethical standards, and as conscientious and responsible as well as anxious and self-critical. As the analyses began, the patients who dropped out were seen as being likeable but were also viewed as feeling ashamed, inadequate, like a failure, and depressed. On the other hand, as the analyses began, patients whose analysis eventually ended because of external events were viewed as enjoying challenges, articulate, able to use their talents productively, and able to recognize alternative viewpoints, as well as feeling guilty. The most common characteristics of patients in the two groups are shown in Table 7.1. These are certainly descriptively different groups.

When we carried out multiple regression analysis of the Shedler–Westen Assessment Procedure (SWAP-200) items of patients in the two groups as

Table 7.1 Shedler–Westen Assessment Procedure (SWAP) items at the beginning of analysis that best describe patients who dropped out of analysis and patients whose analyses ended because of external events

Item	Mean	SD
Dropouts		
092. Is articulate; can express self well in words	5.8	1.9
035. Tends to be anxious	5.0	2.1
068. Appreciates and responds to humor	5.0	1.6
086. Tends to feel ashamed or embarrassed	4.8	2.2
051. Tends to elicit liking in others	4.3	1.6
054. Tends to feel s/he is inadequate, inferior, or a failure	4.3	2.5
091. Tends to be self-critical; sets unrealistically high standards for self and is intolerant of own human defects	4.3	2.3
175. Tends to be conscientious and responsible	4.3	2.3
189. Tends to feel unhappy, depressed, or despondent	4.3	2.2
120. Has moral and ethical standards and strives to live up to them	4.2	1.6
149. Tends to feel like an outcast or outsider; feels as if s/he does not truly belong	4.2	2.0
External events		
175. Tends to be conscientious and responsible	5.7	2.0
019. Enjoys challenges; takes pleasure in accomplishing things	5.1	2.4
092. Is articulate; can express self well in words	5.8	2.5
120. Has moral and ethical standards and strives to live up to them	5.1	2.0
068. Appreciates and responds to humor	4.9	1.8
002. Is able to use his/her talents, abilities, and energy effectively and productively	4.8	2.2
035. Tends to be anxious	4.8	2.5
057. Tends to feel guilty	4.8	2.5
111. Has the capacity to recognize alternative viewpoints, even in matters that stir up strong feelings	4.8	2.1
091. Tends to be self-critical; sets unrealistically high standards for self and is intolerant of own human defects	4.6	2.4

the analyses began, two SWAP-200 items best differentiated between the two groups. As the analyses began, patients who dropped out felt more like outcasts and were less able to hear and use emotionally threatening information than patients whose analyses ended because of external events ($R^2 = 0.36$), shown in Table 7.2.

In stepwise regression analyses, no Personality Disorder Scale scores, Trait Scale scores or adaptive functioning scale scores significantly differentiated between the two groups as the analyses began. In overall comparisons of scale

Table 7.2 Shedler–Westen Assessment Procedure (SWAP) items and scale scores early in analysis that differentiate between patients who dropped out and patients whose analyses ended because of external events

Item	Dropout Mean (SD)	External Mean (SD)	r	R^2	F	p
Predictors of group membership						
SWAP items						
149. Tends to feel like an outcast or outsider; feels as if s/he does not truly belong	4.2 (2.0)	2.2 (1.9)	0.21	0.21	9.72	0.01
082. Is capable of hearing information that is emotionally threatening (i.e., that challenges cherished beliefs, perceptions, and self-perceptions) and can use and benefit from it	2.8 (1.7)	4.4 (1.8)	0.16	0.36	8.79	0.01
Personality Disorder Scales						
None are significant						
Trait Scales						
None are significant						
Adaptive Functioning Scales						
None are significant						

scores as the analyses began, the two attrition groups did not differ in adaptive functioning, Personality Disorder, or Trait Scale scores (Wilks' (3,31) = 0.77, $p = 0.52$, Wilks' (11,25) = 0.31, $p = 0.82$, and Wilks' (10,27) = 0.85, $p = 0.59$, respectively). The SWAP-200 scale and adaptive functioning scores are shown in Figure 7.1.

The patients in five of the analyses that ended for reasons external to the treatment were ethnic minorities; none of the patients who dropped out were ethnic minorities (Wilcoxon $p = 0.003$).

As the analyses began, although more of the patients who ended analysis because of external events than those who ended analysis by dropping out had a graduate or professional education (80% vs. 50%, Wilcoxon $p = 0.03$), this did not reach the required adjusted significance level of $p \leq 0.005$. The two groups did not differ in sex, age, marital status, socioeconomic status, previous treatments, problems with drugs or alcohol, the number of Axis I or Axis II problems, or whether or not they were taking psychotropic medication, with Wilcoxon p values ranging from 0.16 to 0.42.

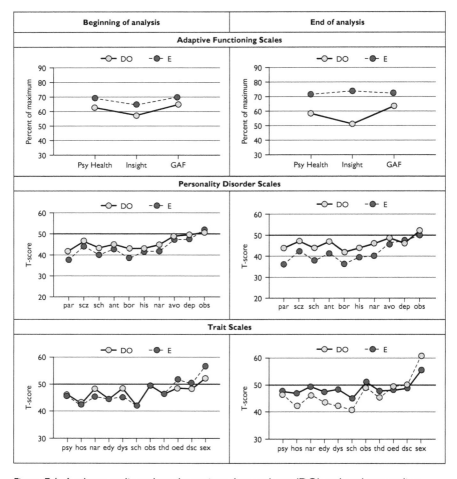

Figure 7.1 Analyses ending when the patient dropped out (DO) and analyses ending because of external events (E) at the beginning and end of analysis

Adaptive Functioning Scales: Psychological Health, Insight, Global Assessment of Functioning (GAF).

Personality Disorder Scales: Paranoid, Schizoid, Schizotypal, Antisocial, Borderline, Histrionic, Narcissistic, Avoidant, Dependent, and Obsessive.

Trait Scales: Psychopathy, Hostility, Narcissism, Emotional Dysregulation, Dysphoria, Schizoid Orientation, Obsessionality, Thought Disorder, Oedipal Conflict, Dissociation, and Sexual Conflict.

Analysts

Although more of the analysts of the patients who dropped out were women – 70% vs. 50%, Wilcoxon $p = 0.03$ – again this did not reach the required adjusted significance level of $p \leq 0.005$. The analysts did not differ in profession, professional experience, or psychoanalytic experience. They did not differ in the theoretical views they endorsed or the number of theoretical views they endorsed (Wilcoxon p ranged from 0.07 to 0.43).

Analyses

The analyses did not differ in frequency (Wilcoxon $p = 0.50$), use of the couch as the analyses began (Wilcoxon $p = 0.27$), or the fee (Wilcoxon $p = 0.50$).

At the end of analysis

Patients

As the analyses ended, patients in both of the attrition groups were described as articulate and conscientious, with moral and ethical standards, responding to humor, and with the capacity to recognize alternative viewpoints. The patients who dropped out, however, although described as insightful, were also described as anxious, feeling inadequate, feeling ashamed, and self-critical. The patients whose analyses ended because of external events, on the other hand, were described as empathic and able to find satisfaction in the pursuit of long-term goals and in nurturing others, but also as having difficulty expressing anger and tending to feel guilty, shown in Table 7.3.

With a multiple regression analysis of the SWAP-200 items as the analyses ended, three SWAP-200 items significantly differentiated between the two groups. As the analyses ended, patients who dropped out were viewed as having less satisfaction in the pursuit of long-term goals, with more tendency to induce their own uncomfortable feelings in others, and as being more arrogant than patients whose analyses ended for reasons external to the treatment ($R^2 = 0.73$). Patients who dropped out also had higher Paranoid Personality Disorder Scale scores than patients whose analyses ended for reasons external to the treatment ($R^2 = 0.21$), and lower scores on the Insight scale ($R^2 = 0.33$). These data are shown in Table 7.4 and Figure 7.1.

Analyses

The two attrition groups did not differ at the end of analysis in the frequency of sessions, the analytic fee, the use of the couch, or the length of analysis. Wilcoxon p ranged from 0.22 to 0.76.

Conclusions

In the direct comparison of the attrition groups in this chapter, as the analyses began, the two attrition groups differed in two SWAP items ($R^2 = 0.36$). As the analyses began, the patients who dropped out were viewed by the analysts as feeling more like outcasts and as being less able to hear emotionally threatening information than the patients whose analyses ended for external reasons. This information should be of very real practical significance in understanding and

Table 7.3 Shedler–Westen Assessment Procedure (SWAP) items at the end of analysis that best describe patients between patients who dropped out of analysis and patients whose analyses ended because of external events

Item	Mean	SD
Dropouts		
092. Is articulate; can express self well in words	5.1	2.0
035. Tends to be anxious	4.8	2.2
054. Tends to feel s/he is inadequate, inferior, or a failure	4.1	2.3
086. Tends to feel ashamed or embarrassed	4.0	2.6
175. Tends to be conscientious and responsible	4.0	2.2
120. Has moral and ethical standards and strives to live up to them	3.9	2.0
068. Appreciates and responds to humor	3.9	2.2
183. Is psychologically insightful; is able to understand self and others in subtle and sophisticated ways	3.8	2.3
091. Tends to be self-critical; sets unrealistically high standards for self and is intolerant of own human defects	3.7	2.6
111. Has the capacity to recognize alternative viewpoints, even in matters that stir up strong feelings	3.6	3.5
External events		
175. Tends to be conscientious and responsible	5.6	2.0
068. Appreciates and responds to humor	5.5	1.9
092. Is articulate; can express self well in words	5.5	2.3
059. Is empathic; is sensitive and responsive to other people's needs and feelings	5.2	1.9
196. Is able to find meaning and satisfaction in the pursuit of long-term goals and ambitions	5.2	1.8
120. Has moral and ethical standards and strives to live up to them	5.1	2.1
055. Is able to find meaning and fulfillment in guiding, mentoring, or nurturing others	5.0	1.8
111. Has the capacity to recognize alternative viewpoints, even in matters that stir up strong feelings	5.0	1.0
025. Has difficulty acknowledging or expressing anger	4.8	2.4
057. Tends to feel guilty	4.8	2.1

helping to reduce some kind of problems that can lead to dropping out. For patients more likely than others to drop out, being in analysis can raise familiar issues of not feeling welcome and these are very likely to be experienced in the relationship with the analyst. This, then, is a type of negative transference. Combined with a heightened sensitivity to hearing about emotionally threatening information, which certainly happens in analytic treatment, the negative transference can make the treatment situation almost intolerable. The data suggest that careful recognition of the patient's feeling like an outcast and working

Table 7.4. Characteristics at the end of analysis that differentiate between patients who dropped out of analysis vs. patients whose analyses ended because of external events

Predictors of group membership	Dropouts Mean (SD)	External events Mean (SD)	r	R^2	F	p
SWAP items						
196. Is able to find meaning and satisfaction in the pursuit of long-term goals and ambitions	2.5 (2.4)	5.3 (1.7)	0.32	0.32	13.83	0.001
076. Manages to elicit in others feelings similar to those he or she is experiencing (e.g., when angry, acts in such a way as to provoke anger in others; when anxious, acts in such a way as to induce anxiety in others)	1.8 (1.6)	0.7 (0.9)	0.23	0.55	14.96	0.001
133. Tends to be arrogant, haughty, or dismissive	1.9 (2.2)	0.3 (0.8)	0.18	0.73	19.21	0.0001
Personality Disorder Scales						
Paranoid	43.2 (2.8)	36.7 (4.9)	0.21	0.21	7.50	0.01
Trait Scales						
None are significant						
Adaptive Functioning Scales						
Insight	51.0 (19.4)	74.0 (13.2)	0.33	0.33	14.57	0.001

SWAP, Shedler–Westen Assessment Procedure.

with these feelings in the transference, and careful dosing of interpretations regarding emotionally threatening material may very well reduce the likelihood that the vulnerable patient will drop out of treatment.

Of the six patients in the study who were ethnic minorities, the analyses of five ended for reasons external to the treatment and none of these patients dropped out. The sixth analysis ended with maximum benefits. Three of the five patients whose analyses ended for reasons external to the treatment had a graduate or professional education when they began treatment; the analyst of one of these three relocated. One of the five completed college more than a year before the analysis ended when the analyst relocated. Why minority group members left for external reasons is not clear and certainly warrants further exploration.

As the analyses ended, in the direct comparison of the two attrition groups, patients whose analyses ended because of external events were viewed as being healthier – e.g., they were more satisfied in pursuing long-term goals, more insightful, and less paranoid – than patients who dropped out. Patients whose analyses ended because of external events had lower scores at the end of analysis on a SWAP-200 item about eliciting in others uncomfortable feelings similar to those they were feeling, an immature defense against uncomfortable feelings related to higher levels of paranoia. Patients whose analyses ended because of external events also had lower scores at the end of analysis on a SWAP-200 item about being arrogant, perhaps because they had less need to defend against the uncomfortable rigors of analysis by magnifying more narcissistic features such as arrogance.

We are left with unanswered questions, of course. A tremendous range of situations can interrupt an analysis and differences between these situations certainly must matter and may well be worth exploring. Several analysts who were participating in the project relocated. We know little about the situations where analysts relocate and can imagine that the analyst in this situation may, perhaps, have seen the analysis as more complete and the analysands as healthier than would have been the case were it not for their move. On the other hand, in one of the analyses, the analyst died and in another a patient became critically ill. Analysis is not a panacea for all of life's problems. What we can note is the patient who graduates from college or completes graduate school and must move may well be and be seen as successful and ready to make what is really a planned ending of an incomplete analysis. On the other hand, the present data do support the finding that dropping out of analysis is related to less positive features at both the beginning and end of analysis than attrition because of reasons external to the treatment and that the recognizing characteristics of patients who are more likely to drop out than other patients may well be clinically useful.

References

Freud, S. (1909). A case of obsessional neurosis. In J. Stracey (Ed. and transl.), *The standard edition of the complete psychological works of Sigmund Freud* (Vol. 9). London: Hogarth Press, pp. 155–249. (Reprinted in 1981.)

Westmacott, R., & Hunsley, J. (2010). Reasons for terminating psychotherapy: A general population study. *Journal of Clinical Psychology, 66(9),* 965–977.

Chapter 8

Analyses ending with mutual agreement between patient and analyst

Without maximum benefits vs. others

> In a treatment which is incomplete or in which success is not perfect,
> one may at any rate achieve a considerable improvement.
>
> (Freud, 1904/1981, p. 253)

Introduction

Analytic outcomes certainly are not just a dichotomy: success or failure, excellent results or no help at all, good or bad. Part of our goal in the present work is to understand more about a range of outcomes. Here we consider only studies of analyses that were considered complete, ending with mutual agreement between the patient and analyst, but without maximum benefits. It is not entirely clear what the terms mean in the relevant studies in the literature we review below but we will proceed and see what we can learn.

Of the 60 analyses in our study, 6 (10%) ended with mutual agreement between patient and analyst but without maximum benefits in the view of the analyst. Here we will consider characteristics at the beginning of analysis that predict analyses agreement between patient and analyst but without maximum benefits vs. other analyses. We will also consider what characteristics at the end of analysis differentiate between patients ending without maximum benefits and other patients. As we have done in considering other outcomes of psychoanalysis in the preceding chapters, we begin by reviewing the theoretical literature on ideas about why some people have maximum benefits from psychoanalysis and psychotherapy.

Prevalence and predictors of outcomes without maximum benefits in psychoanalysis and psychotherapy

Psychoanalysis

We found eight studies of psychoanalytic outcome that considered analyses ending with mutual agreement between analyst and patient and differentiated between analyses with the patient apparently cured or much improved and analyses in which the patient was much improved but not cured. In an early study, Coriat (1917) considered the results of 93 completed cases and reported that 49% were "recovered" and another 41% had positive results but were not in the recovered group. In Knight's (1941) composite report of 660 analyses that continued for 6 months or longer, 56% of the patients were cured or much improved and 30% were improved. We might assume that the 30% identified as improved is the relevant outcome group in terms of being without maximum benefits. In a series of papers concerning patients analyzed by analysts in training at the New York or Boston Psychoanalytic Institutes, only from 6% (Erle & Goldberg, 1984) to 10% (Bachrach, Weber, & Solomon, 1985; Weber, Bachrach, & Solomon, 1985a, 1985b) of applicants for analysis were selected. The New York and Boston Institute studies described the results of 387 analyses of these highly selected patients: 40% ended with maximum benefits and 32% ended with mutual agreement and were improved but not with maximum benefits. In the Menninger project (cf. Wallerstein, 1986), of 22 analyses that were complete, 36% had maximum benefits and 36% were improved but did not have maximum benefits. Finally, Luborsky et al. (2001) reported on 17 complete analyses that were recorded and transcribed and found that 12% had maximum benefits and 41% were improved but without maximum benefits. While there are certainly very real differences between these studies, of 1,179 analyses, 32% ended with mutual agreement and with the analysands viewed as improved but without maximum benefits. The only predictor of the extent of benefits, identified in studies from the Boston Psychoanalytic Institute, was the length of treatments; analyses with better outcomes were longer (Bachrach et al., 1985; Weber et al., 1985a, 1985b).

Psychotherapy

Our plan here is to consider psychotherapy outcome studies that differentiated between outcomes in which the patient was cured or had maximum benefits vs. outcomes in which the patient was much improved or improved. This limit severely restricts the relevant literature.

Behavior therapy

Although Wolpe (1967, 1969) explicitly followed Knight's (1941) categories, he combined patients who were apparently recovered and patients who were at least 80% improved into a single group. Lazarus (1963) reported on behavior therapy in 126 of his patients with a severe neurosis. The 126 patients included adults seen for six or more sessions, where therapy did not end because of external factors. Although the results are very clear on the one hand – 19% were completely recovered, 43% were markedly improved, 18% were slightly improved, and 21% were unimproved – this becomes more difficult to sort out when we learn that the 126 were from 408 patients who consulted Lazarus. Lazarus noted that 321 of the 408 patients who consulted appeared to have improved.

Psychodynamic psychotherapy

Several investigators have considered the outcomes of psychodynamic psycho-therapy. In the Menninger project (cf. Wallerstein, 1986), of 20 patients in psychotherapy, 45% had what was described as really good improvement and 30% had moderate or equivocal improvement. Luborsky, Crits-Christoph, Mintz, and Auerbach (1988) reported on the outcomes of psychodynamic therapy in 73 patients who completed psychotherapy either in clinic or private practice settings in the Penn [Pennsylvania] Psychotherapy Project. Based on reports of therapists, 22% of the patients showed large global improvement, 43% showed moderate improvement, 27% showed some improvement, 7% showed no change, and 1% were worse at the end of psychotherapy. Only the length of psychotherapy or number of sessions had a major predictive role in the psychotherapy outcomes. Luborsky et al. (1988) note that whether this is because more therapy leads to better outcomes or because healthier patients are able to stay in therapy longer is not clear.

The present cases without maximum benefits

As the analyses began

Patients

Three of the six patients who ended analysis without maximum benefits were women and three were men. Their average age was 39.7 years (SD = 13.6). Five were married or in a committed relationship and one was single. Three were viewed as middle class, one as upper-middle class, and two as upper class. One had some college, three had completed college, and two had a graduate or professional education. All six patients had an Axis I clinical diagnosis, including three with anxiety and three with depression. Four had an Axis II clinical diagnosis, including one each with Histrionic, Obsessive, or Self-Defeating Personality Disorder and one with Personality Disorder Not Otherwise Specified. Two had possible alcohol problems and none had drug problems. All six were taking psychotropic medication, including five taking antidepressant, two taking antianxiety, and one taking antipsychotic medication. Three had been in previous treatment. One had a previous psychiatric hospitalization.

The Shedler–Westen Assessment Procedure (SWAP) items most characteristic of patients without maximum benefits and other patients at the beginning of analysis are shown in Table 8.1. Patients in both groups were seen as having moral and ethical standards, being conscientious, self-critical, and articulate, feeling guilty, and appreciating humor. Beyond this, patients who ended analysis with mutual agreement between analyst and patient but without maximum benefits were insightful and found meaning in contributing to a larger community but were also suggestible and inhibited about pursuing goals. Other patients were viewed as likeable, empathic, competitive,

Table 8.1 Shedler–Westen Assessment Procedure (SWAP) items at the beginning of analysis that best describe patients who finished without maximum benefits vs. others

Item	Mean	SD
Without maximum benefits		
037. Finds meaning in belong and contributing to a larger community (e.g., organization, church, neighborhood, etc.)	5.0	1.4
120. Has moral and ethical standards and strives to live up to them	4.8	1.2
046. Tends to be suggestible or easily influenced	4.7	1.4
033. Appears inhibited about pursuing goals or successes; aspirations or achievements tend to be below his/her potential	4.3	3.4
057. Tends to feel guilty	4.3	2.4
068. Appreciates and responds to humor	4.2	2.9
092. Is articulate, can express self well in words	4.2	2.2
091. Tends to be self-critical; sets unrealistically high standards for self and is intolerant of own human defects	4.0	2.0
175. Tends to be conscientious and responsible	4.0	2.6
183. Is psychologically insightful; is able to understand self and others in subtle and sophisticated ways	4.0	2.1
Others		
092. Is articulate; can express self well in words	5.6	2.0
175. Tends to be conscientious and responsible	5.0	2.2
035. Tends to be anxious	4.9	2.3
068. Appreciates and responds to humor	4.8	1.8
091. Tends to be self-critical; sets unrealistically high standards for self and is intolerant of own human defects	4.8	2.2
120. Has moral and ethical standards and strives to live up to them	4.8	1.7
057. Tends to feel guilty	4.5	2.6
051. Tends to elicit liking in others	4.4	1.8
059. Is empathic; is sensitive and responsive to other people's needs and feelings	4.5	1.9
084. Tends to be competitive with others (whether consciously or unconsciously)	3.9	2.1

Table 8.2 Shedler–Westen Assessment Procedure (SWAP) items and scale scores at the beginning of analysis that differentiate between patients without maximum benefits (MB) and others

Predictors of group membership	Without MB Mean (SD)	Others Mean (SD)	r	R²	F	p
SWAP items						
046. Tends to be suggestible or easily influenced	4.7 (1.4)	1.7 (1.9)	0.19	0.19	13.51	0.0005
188. Work life tends to be chaotic or unstable (e.g., working arrangements seem always temporary, transitional, or ill defined)	2.5 (2.9)	0.6 (1.4)	0.10	0.30	8.30	0.006
Personality Disorder Scales						
None are significant						
Trait Scales						
None are significant						
Adaptive Functioning Scales						
None are significant						

and anxious. From a stepwise regression analysis, the individual SWAP items and scale scores that best differentiated between the patients without maximum benefits and other patients are shown in Table 8.2. At the beginning of analysis, patients who finished analysis without maximum benefits tended to be more suggestible than other patients, and seemed to have more chaotic work lives than others ($R^2 = 0.30$). No SWAP personality disorder, trait, or adaptive functioning scale scores significantly differentiated between the patients whose analyses ended without maximum benefits and other patients, shown in Figure 8.1.

We explored differences in the characteristics of patients whose analyses ended without maximum benefits and other patients with a series of non-parametric analyses. Only previous psychiatric hospitalization differed significantly between the two groups (Wilcoxon $p = 0.005$). One person in the group without maximum benefits and none of the other patients had a previous psychiatric hospitalization. As the analyses began, all six of the patients whose analyses ended without maximum benefits and 24 of the other 30 patients (44.4%) were taking psychotropic medication (Wilcoxon $p = 0.02$), which did not reach the necessary adjusted significance level of 0.005. Aside from these characteristics, Wilcoxon p ranged from 0.05 to 0.88.

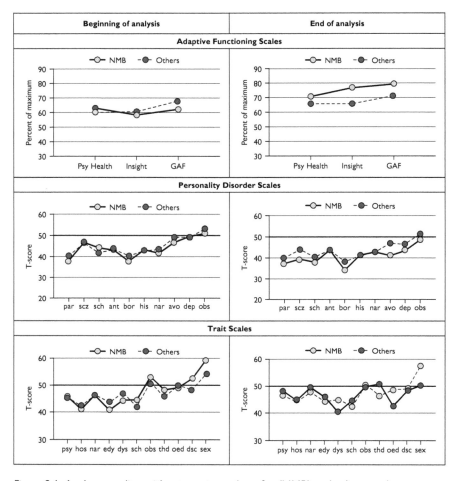

Figure 8.1 Analyses ending without maximum benefits (NMB) and others at the
beginning and end of analysis

Adaptive Functioning Scales: Psychological Health, Insight, Global Assessment of Functioning (GAF).

Personality Disorder Scales: Paranoid, Schizoid, Schizotypal, Antisocial, Borderline, Histrionic,
Narcissistic, Avoidant, Dependent, and Obsessive.

Trait Scales: Psychopathy, Hostility, Narcissism, Emotional Dysregulation, Dysphoria, Schizoid
Orientation, Obsessionality, Thought Disorder, Oedipal Conflict, Dissociation, and Sexual Conflict.

Analysts

Four of the analysts whose patients ended analysis without maximum benefits
were men and two were women. Three were psychiatrists, one was a psychologist, and two were social workers. They had an average of 20.3 years of professional experience (sd = 9.5) and 10.3 years of psychoanalytic experience

(SD = 6.1). For all six analysts, object relations theory was a primary theoretical orientation. Three also endorsed ego psychology, two endorsed drive/conflict theory, and one endorsed self-psychology. Characteristics of the analysts of the patients who ended analyses without maximum benefits and others did not differ significantly. Wilcoxon *p* values ranged from 0.04 to 1.00.

Analyses

Of the six analyses without maximum benefits, two were three times a week and four were four times a week. As the analyses began, three patients were on the couch, one was generally on the couch, and one was not on the couch. The fees varied and included two patients who paid a full fee, three who paid 75% of a full fee, and one who paid 50% of a full fee.

The average length of the analyses ending with the mutual agreement of patient and analyst without maximum benefits was 55.2 months (SD = 23.0). As the analyses began, fewer of the patients whose analyses ended without maximum benefits than other patients were on the couch: 50% vs. 80% of other patients (Wilcoxon *p* = 0.02), which does reach the required adjusted level of statistical significance. We do not know whether this reflects caution on the part of the analysts or reluctance on the part of the patients, although given the items that predicted membership in the not maximum benefits outcome group, we suspect the difference reflects caution on the part of the analysts. In other comparisons, Wilcoxon *p* ranged from 0.30 to 0.58.

As the analyses ended

Patients

As the analyses ended, one patient whose analysis ended without maximum benefits had possible alcohol problems and one had possible drug problems. Medication use had changed somewhat: two patients rather than four were taking antidepressant medication; one was still taking antianxiety medication and one was still taking antipsychotic medication. Wilcoxon *p* values ranged from 0.14 to 0.49.

As the analyses ended, 49 of the analysts provided SWAP data as well as questionnaire responses. The most descriptive SWAP items as the analyses ended are shown in Table 8.3. The most characteristic items describing patients who ended analysis with mutual agreement between patient and analyst but without maximum benefits were all positive while the characteristics of the other patients were mixed. With a multiple regression analysis, three items differentiated between the two groups, shown in Table 8.4. At the end of analysis, patients ending with mutual agreement but not maximum benefits were viewed as tending to seek thrills more than others, having more exaggerated expression of qualities or mannerisms associated with their own sex than others, and as seeming less naïve or innocent than others ($R^2 = 0.56$).

Table 8.3 Shedler–Westen Assessment Procedure (SWAP) items at the end of analysis that best describe patients who finished without maximum benefits and others

Item	Mean	SD
Without maximum benefits		
068. Appreciates and responds to humor	6.2	0.9
032. Is capable of sustaining a meaningful love relationship characterized by genuine intimacy and sharing	6.0	0.9
019. Enjoys challenges; takes pleasure in accomplishing things	6.0	1.5
200. Is able to form close and lasting friendships characterized by mutual support and sharing of experiences	5.8	1.5
037. Finds meaning in belonging and contributing to a larger community (e.g., organization, church, neighborhood, etc.)	5.5	2.0
089. Appears to have come to terms with painful experiences from the past; has found meaning in, and grown from such experiences	5.5	1.4
002. Is able to use his/her talents, abilities, and energy effectively and productively	5.3	1.6
063. Is able to assert him/herself effectively and appropriately when necessary	5.2	0.8
183. Is psychologically insightful; is able to understand self and others in subtle and sophisticated ways	5.2	2.2
059. Is empathic; is sensitive and responsive to other people's needs and feelings	5.0	1.8
Others		
092. Is articulate; can express self well in words	5.3	2.2
175. Tends to be conscientious and responsible	4.8	2.4
035. Tends to be anxious	4.7	2.0
068. Appreciates and responds to humor	4.5	2.3
120. Has moral and ethical standards and strives to live up to them	4.5	2.2
183. Is psychologically insightful; is able to understand self and others in subtle and sophisticated ways	4.4	2.4
084. Tends to be competitive with others (whether consciously or unconsciously)	4.1	2.1
111. Has the capacity to recognize alternative viewpoints, even in matters that stir up strong feelings	4.1	2.3
019. Enjoys challenges; takes pleasure in accomplishing things	3.9	2.5
057. Tends to feel guilty	3.8	2.3

Table 8.4 Shedler–Westen Assessment Procedure (SWAP) items, and scale scores at the end of analysis that differentiate between patients who finished without maximum benefits (MB) and others

Predictors of group membership	Without MB Mean (SD)	Others Mean (SD)	r	R²	F	p
SWAP items						
071. Tends to seek thrills, novelty, adventure, etc.	2.5 (2.3)	0.4 (0.8)	0.31	0.31	21.46	<0.0001
107. Tends to express qualities or mannerisms traditionally associated with own sex to an exaggerated degree (i.e., a hyperfeminine woman or a hypermasculine, "macho" man)	1.8 (2.5)	0.3 (1.0)	0.15	0.46	12.61	0.001
093. Seems to know less about the ways of the world than might be expected, given his/her intelligence, background, etc.; appears naïve or innocent	1.0 (2.0)	2.4 (2.2)	0.10	0.56	9.81	0.003
Personality Disorder Scales						
None are significant						
Trait Scales						
None are significant						
Adaptive Functioning Scales						
None are significant						

Analyses

The analyses of the six patients whose analyses ended with mutual agreement between patient and analyst and without maximum benefits were longer than those of the 54 other patients, with an average of 55.2 months (SD = 23.0) vs. 32.7 months (SD = 27.5), Wilcoxon $p = 0.04$ which, again, approaches but does not reach the required adjusted level of statistical significance for these comparisons of characteristics of the analyses, which was $p \leq 0.02$.

Conclusions

At the beginning of analysis, the picture of people who ended analysis with mutual agreement between analyst and patient and without maximum benefits was of positive features but with some limitations. The SWAP items that best predicted patients likely to end analysis without maximum benefits may suggest a more impulsive and less than ideally thought-through entry into analysis: They tended to be suggestible or easily influenced, with a more chaotic work life than others. The R^2 of 0.30 is not trivial.

At the end of analysis, the SWAP items that best differentiated between patients who ended analysis without maximum benefits and others are also not transparent. At the end of analysis, patients without maximum benefits were seen as more inclined than others to be thrill seekers, more hypermasculine or hyperfeminine than others, and appeared less naïve than others ($R^2 = 0.56$). We might see the changes from the beginning to the end of analysis as reflecting an increase in a kind of freedom, as an increase in adolescent characteristics, or perhaps – given that they appear somewhat *less* naïve than others as the analyses end —as having a degree of hiding or obscuring parts of themselves. We ask the reader to withhold more judgment until we consider the characteristics of people who complete analysis with maximum benefits.

References

Bachrach, H. M., Weber, J. J., & Solomon, M. (1985). Factors associated with the outcome of psychoanalysis (clinical and methodological considerations): Report of the Columbia Psychoanalytic Center Research Project (IV). *International Review of Psycho-Analysis, 12,* 379–388.

Coriat, I. H. (1917). Some statistical results of the psychoanalytic treatment of the psychoneuroses. *Psychoanalytic Review, 4,* 209–216.

Erle, J. B., & Goldberg, D. A. (1984). Observations on assessment of analyzability by experienced analysts. *Journal of the American Psychoanalytic Association, 32,* 715–737.

Freud, S. (1904). Freud's psychoanalytic procedure. In J. Strachey (Ed. and transl.), *The standard edition of the complete psychological works of Sigmund Freud* (Vol. 7). London: Hogarth Press, pp. 249–254. (Reprinted in 1981.)

Knight, R. P. (1941). Evaluation of the results of psychoanalytic therapy. *American Journal of Psychiatry, 98,* 434–446.

Lazarus. A. A. (1963). The results of behavior therapy in 126 cases of severe neurosis. *Behavior Research and Therapy, 1,* 69–80.

Luborsky, L., Crits-Christoph, P., Mintz, J., & Auerbach, A. (1988). *Who will benefit from psychotherapy? Predicting therapeutic outcomes.* New York: Basic Books.

Luborsky, L., Stuart, J., Friedman, S., Diguer, L., Seligman, D. A., Bucci, W., Pulver, S., Krause, E. D., Ermold, J., Daavison, W. T., Woody, G., & Mergenthaler, E. (2001). The Penn Psychoanalytic Treatment Collection: A set of complete and recorded psychoanalyses as a research resource. *Journal of the American Psychoanalytic Association, 49,* 217–234.

Wallerstein, R. S. (1986). *Forty-two lives in treatment: A study of psychoanalysis and psychotherapy.* New York: Guilford Press.

Weber, J. J., Bachrach, H. M., & Solomon, M. (1985a). Factors associated with the outcome of psychoanalysis: Report of the Columbia Psychoanalytic Center research project (II). *International Review of Psychoanalysis, 12,* 127–141.

Weber, J. J., Bachrach, H. M., & Solomon, M. (1985b). Factors associated with the outcome of psychoanalysis: Report of the Columbia Psychoanalytic Center research project (III). *International Review of Psychoanalysis, 12*, 251–262.

Wolpe, J. (1967). Behavior therapy and psychotherapeutic goals. In A. R. Mahrer (Ed.), *The goals of psychotherapy*. New York: Appleton-Century-Crofts, pp. 129–144.

Wolpe, J. (1969). *The practice of behavior therapy*. New York: Pergamon.

Chapter 9

Analyses ending with mutual agreement between patient and analyst

With maximum benefits vs. others

> One can live magnificently in this world if one knows how to work and how to love.
>
> (Tolstoy, 1954)

Introduction

Perhaps Freud said that the goals of analysis are to be able to work and love. These splendid words are not in his writings but were attributed to Freud by Erikson in *Childhood and Society* (Erikson, 1950/1963, pp. 264–265). Freud wrote with feeling about the goals of analysis as having to do with the "restoration of [the patient's] ability to lead an active life and of his capacity for enjoyment" (Freud, 1904/1981, p. 253). Of the 60 analyses in the study, of which 17 ended with the agreement of patient and analyst, 11 (18.3%) ended with maximum benefits in the view of the analyst.

Here we want to know two things about the best outcomes of analysis. First, we want to know what people likely to have maximum benefits are like as the analysis begins. If we knew more about this, perhaps we would have an idea of how to be most helpful to someone who begins analysis without the key characteristics. We might modify our analytic conversation or we might modify our goals. The Shedler–Westen Assessment Procedure (SWAP) should also provide a practical and meaningful description of someone at the end of an analysis with maximum benefits. This description will give us new information about what contemporary psychoanalysts mean when they identify someone as having had maximum benefits from analysis.

As we have done in considering other outcomes of psychoanalysis in the preceding chapters, we begin by reviewing the theoretical literature on ideas about why some people have maximum benefits from psychoanalysis and psychotherapy. We also review the limited empirical literature reporting the prevalence and predictors of maximum benefits from psychoanalysis and psychotherapy. We then look closely at the analyses in this project as they began and as they ended to see what differentiated patients, analysts, and analyses with maximum benefits.

Ideas about who has maximum benefits in psychoanalysis and psychotherapy

Psychoanalysis

Freud proposed that analysis was most effective with people who were intelligent (1895/1981, 1905/1981), educated (1905/1981), less than 50 years old (1904/1981), and psychologically healthier than others (Freud, 1937/1981). He thought that analysis was less effective with people who were psychotic, paranoid, or had drug problems (1905/1981). Subsequent theorists have focused on three characteristics thought to be associated with analyzability: an ability to form relationships (Lower, Escoll & Huxster, 1972; Sandler, Holder, & Dare, 1970; Zetzel, 1965), hysteria (Fenichel, 1945; Glover, 1954; Jones, 1920; Lower et al., 1972; Zetzel, 1965), and psychological mindedness (Abrams, 1992; Lower et al., 1972).

Psychotherapy

The literature about who is most likely to benefit from psychotherapy is difficult to find, with a few exceptions somewhat related to the problem. The very idea that some people might benefit from psychotherapy more than others is offensive to some psychotherapists today. However, Rogers' (1957) list of six "psychological conditions which are both necessary and sufficient to bring about constructive personality change" (p. 96) included one characteristic of the client. The client, said Rogers, must be "in a state of incongruence, being vulnerable or anxious" (p. 96). Schofield (1964) proposed that therapists expect patients who are youthful, attractive, verbal, intelligent, and successful to do best in psychotherapy, termed YAVIS by Schofield (1964, p. 133). While therapists' expectations are not the same as the patient's response to psychotherapy, Schofield's proposal does suggest that psychotherapists have views of "success" in psychotherapy.

Prevalence and predictors of outcomes with maximum benefits in psychoanalysis and psychotherapy

Psychoanalysis

Studies of the outcome of psychoanalysis go back to 1917, when Coriat reviewed 93 of his completed cases and reported that 46 (49%) were cured. For people with severe problems, the treatments lasted for 4–6 months! In 1941, Knight summarized reports of completed cases from around the world, including the Berlin Institute, a US private practice group, the London Clinic, the Chicago Institute, and the Menninger Clinic. Of 660 analyses that had continued for 6 months or longer, 183 (28%) were "apparently cured." At the

Columbia Clinic, a psychoanalytic training clinic, 66% of 77 patients who ended analysis as private patients of their psychoanalysts had maximum benefits, compared with 26% of 158 patients who ended as clinic patients (Weber, Bachrach, & Solomon, 1985). In a second Columbia Clinic sample, 56% of 16 patients who ended analysis as private patients and 15% of 20 who ended as clinic patients had maximum benefits (Bachrach, 1993).

We found some studies of characteristics of patients at the beginning of psychoanalysis that predicted maximum benefits. Luborsky et al. (2001) grouped 17 completed analyses that had been audiotape-recorded into two "top cases" (12%), nine with intermediate benefits, and six that were essentially unimproved. Luborsky had worked with the Menninger project and noted that the results were similar to the outcomes of the Menninger project. The 22 completed psychoanalyses in the Menninger project, involving very difficult cases, included eight with "very good" outcomes (36%), five with "moderate" outcomes, and six that were "failures." Luborsky et al. (2001) reported that patients with better functioning at the beginning of analysis had better outcomes than other patients, although the authors noted that the raters did not agree on the functioning of the patients at the beginning of analysis.

These studies show that analysts view some analyses as ending with particularly positive results. The literature provides very little understanding of what predicts outcomes with maximum benefits or what patients with maximum benefits are like at the end of analysis.

Psychotherapy

There have been literally thousands of studies of the effectiveness of psychotherapy, with quite a few major reviews of the literature (cf. Shedler, 2010). However, there are few studies of a range of psychotherapy outcomes from poor to much improved. Psychological health as psychotherapy begins has been related to better outcomes (cf. Castonguay & Beutler, 2006; Luborsky, Auerbach, Chandler, Cohen, & Bachrach, 1971; Luborsky, Crits-Christoph, Mintz, & Auerbach, 1988; Luborsky, Diguer, et al., 1993; Luborsky, Docherty, Miller, & Barber, 1993; Luborsky & Spence, 1971). Having a higher educational level (Luborsky & Spence, 1971), less impairment, and not having employment and/or financial problems at the beginning of psychotherapy also predicted a better likelihood of benefiting from psychotherapy (Castonguay & Beutler, 2006).

Behavior therapy

Wolpe (1958) reported that, of 210 people he treated with behavior therapy, 39% were apparently cured, 50.5% were much improved, 7.2% were slightly to moderately improved, and 3.3% were unimproved. He regarded the last three categories as, quite simply, failures. The 88 patients treated most recently in the 1958 series were in therapy for an average of 10.7 months with an average of 45.6 interviews. Based on all patients of the patients seen by Wolpe, a 65% recovery rate might describe his results rather than the 89.5% Wolpe reported.

Psychodynamic psychotherapy

The therapists in Luborsky et al.'s (1988) study of people in psychotherapy reported that 16 (22%) of the 73 patients were much improved. Improvement was related to the length of treatment ($r = 0.27$) and the authors noted that this might mean either that more therapy was helpful or that people able to stay in therapy for a longer period of time were healthier as therapy began, which might be related to better outcomes.

The present cases with and without maximum benefits

As the analyses began

Patients

Five of the 11 patients with maximum benefits in the longitudinal project were men and six were women. Their average age was 37.2 years ($sd = 11.0$). Eight were married or in a committed relationship; three were not. One had some college, three had a college education and seven had a graduate or professional education. Five were middle class, three were upper-middle class, and one was upper class. Nine had an Axis I clinical diagnosis, including four with depression, two with anxiety, two with mixed anxiety and depression, and one with separation anxiety. Six had an Axis II clinical diagnosis, including one with a diagnosis of Obsessive, one with Histrionic, and one with Avoidant Personality Disorder, and three with a diagnosis of Personality Disorder Not Otherwise Specified. One patient had alcohol problems, one had possible alcohol problems, one had drug problems, and one had possible drug problems. As the analyses began, four were taking psychotropic medication(s), including three taking antidepressant medication, two antianxiety medication, and two another psychotropic medication. Five had been in treatment before. We explored differences in the characteristics of patients whose analyses ended with maximum benefits and others with a series of non-parametric analyses. No background characteristics of the patients significantly differentiated between the two groups. Wilcoxon p ranged from 0.15 to 0.94.

In terms of the picture from individual SWAP items as the analyses began, people in both groups had a great deal in common, as can be seen in Table 9.1. People in both groups were viewed as empathic, likeable, conscientious, and articulate, with moral and ethical standards they tried to live up to. People in both groups were also described as anxious and self-critical with feelings of guilt. People who had maximum benefits from analysis were viewed as having difficulty expressing anger and as able to form close and lasting friendships. People who did not have maximum benefits were described as articulate people able to appreciate humor and able to recognize alternative viewpoints.

To consider patient factors at the beginning of analysis that best differentiated people with maximum benefits from others, we carried out four stepwise multiple regression analyses considering SWAP items, Personality Disorder Scales, Trait Scales, and adaptive functioning scores. One SWAP item at the beginning of analysis differentiated between the two groups. Patients who had maximum benefits had higher scores on a SWAP item concerned with order,

Table 9.1 Shedler–Westen Assessment Procedure (SWAP) items at the beginning of analysis that best describe patients with maximum benefits and others

Item	Mean	SD
With maximum benefits		
120. Has moral and ethical standards and strives to live up to them	5.8	1.1
175. Tends to be conscientious and responsible	5.8	2.0
092. Is articulate; can express self well in words	5.7	1.3
059. Is empathic; is sensitive and responsive to other people's needs and feelings	5.5	1.9
091. Tends to be self-critical; sets unrealistically high standards for self and is intolerant of own human defects	5.5	1.9
051. Tends to elicit liking in others	5.4	1.4
057. Tends to feel guilty	5.3	2.0
025. Has difficulty acknowledging or expressing anger	5.2	1.2
035. Tends to be anxious	5.2	1.9
200. Is able to form close and lasting friendships characterized by mutual support and sharing of experiences	5.0	2.0
Others		
092. Is articulate; can express self well in words	5.4	2.2
035. Tends to be anxious	4.7	2.4
068. Appreciates and responds to humor	4.7	1.9
120. Has moral and ethical standards and strives to live up to them	4.6	1.7
175. Tends to be conscientious and responsible	4.7	2.3
091. Tends to be self-critical; sets unrealistically high standards for self and is intolerant of own human defects	4.5	2.3
057. Tends to feel guilty	4.2	2.6
059. Is empathic; is sensitive and responsive to other people's needs and feelings	4.1	1.9
051. Tends to elicit liking in others	4.1	2.0
111. Has the capacity to recognize alternative viewpoints, even in matters that stir up strong feelings	4.0	1.9

organization, and schedules ($R^2 = 0.16$). The average score on this item among analysands who ended analysis with maximum benefits was 6.2 (SD = 0.7), with a score of 7 as the highest possible score in the SWAP item ratings, as compared with an average score of 2.5 (SD = 2.5) for others beginning analysis. As the analyses began, the SWAP Personality Disorder Scale scores, SWAP Trait Scale scores, and the adaptive functioning scores did not differentiate significantly between the groups in the multiple regression analyses. However, the groups differed overall on both the Personality Disorder and Trait Scale scores – Wilks' $F(10, 48) = 2.04$, $p = 0.05$ and Wilks' $F(11, 46) = 2.36$, $p = 0.02$ respectively. As the analyses began, patients who had maximum benefits had lower scores on the Antisocial Personality Disorder Scale, $F(1,57) = 5.24$, $p = 0.03$; lower scores on the Narcissism Trait scale, $F(1,56) = 4.47$, $p = 0.04$; and higher scores on the Obsessiveness Trait Scale, $F(1,56) = 4.55$, $p = 0.04$. At the beginning of analysis, the adaptive functioning scores of patients with and without maximum benefits did not differ significantly, Wilks' $F(3,51) = 1.38$, $p = 0.26$. The SWAP scale and adaptive functioning scores are shown in Figure 9.1.

Analysts

Nine of the 11 analysts whose patients had a maximum benefit were women and two were men. They had an average of 24.1 years of professional experience (SD = 10.3) and 10.5 years of psychoanalytic experience (SD = 9.1). Five were psychiatrists, two were psychologists, two were social workers, and two were not psychiatrists, psychologists, or social workers. Their primary theoretical orientations were most often drive theory and object relations theory,

Table 9.2 Shedler–Westen Assessment Procedure (SWAP) items and scale scores at the beginning of analysis that differentiate between patients with maximum benefits (MB) and others

Predictors of group membership	MB Mean (SD)	Other Mean (SD)	Partial R^2	Model R^2	F	p
SWAP items						
192. Tends to be overly concerned with rules, procedures, order, organization, schedules, etc.	3.8 (2.3)	1.6 (2.0)	0.16	0.16	10.46	0.002
Personality Disorder Scales						
None are significant						
Trait Scales						
None are significant						
Adaptive Functioning Scales						
None are significant						

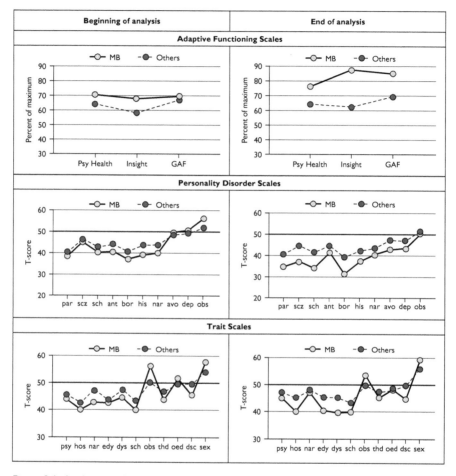

Figure 9.1 Analyses ending with maximum benefits (MB) and others at the beginning and end of analysis

Adaptive Functioning Scales: Psychological Health, Insight, Global Assessment of Functioning (GAF).

Personality Disorder Scales: Paranoid, Schizoid, Schizotypal, Antisocial, Borderline, Histrionic, Narcissistic, Avoidant, Dependent, and Obsessive.

Trait Scales: Psychopathy, Hostility, Narcissism, Emotional Dysregulation, Dysphoria, Schizoid Orientation, Obsessionality, Thought Disorder, Oedipal Conflict, Dissociation, and Sexual Conflict.

each identified by eight analysts. Six said that ego psychology was a primary theoretical orientation, two said self-psychology, and four said other views. No characteristics of the analysts of patients whose analyses ended with maximum benefits and others were significantly different. Wilcoxon p values ranged from 0.15 to 0.89.

Analyses

Of the 11 analyses with a maximum benefit, ten were four times a week and one was three times a week. All were on the couch in a private practice setting. The fees paid for analysis varied and included three patients who paid 100% of the analyst's full fee, three who paid 75%, three who paid 50%, and two who paid 25% of a full fee. The two groups did not differ in characteristics of the analyses. Wilcoxon p values ranged from 0.14 to 0.80.

As the analyses ended

Patients

Among the patients whose analyses ended with maximum benefits, as the analyses ended two patients had a college education and nine had a graduate or professional education; seven were married or in a committed relationship, two were divorced and two were single; one patient still had alcohol problems; drug and possible alcohol problems of two other patients had been resolved. One of the patients with maximum benefits was taking antidepressant medication and two were taking antianxiety medication. At the end of analysis, the patients with maximum benefits and others did not differ in education or other characteristics. Wilcoxon p ranged from 0.07 to 0.86.

As the analyses ended, 49 analysts provided SWAP data as well as questionnaire responses. The most descriptive SWAP items of patients in both groups are shown in Table 9.3. As the analyses were ending, patients from both groups were seen as enjoying challenges, empathic, articulate, and conscientious, with moral and ethical standards and as insightful. People with maximum benefits were also seen as able to sustain a meaningful love relationship and maintain close friendships, to have come to terms with painful experiences from the past, and to be able to express affect appropriately. On the other hand, as their analyses ended, people without maximum benefits were seen as anxious, self-critical, feeling guilty, and tending to be competitive with others.

Stepwise regression analysis showed that the SWAP item that best differentiated between the two groups at the end of analysis was having come to terms with the past ($R^2 = 0.32$), shown in Table 9.4. As the analyses ended, in terms of the SWAP scale scores, people whose analyses ended with maximum benefits had lower Paranoid Personality Disorder Scale scores ($R^2 = 0.17$), and higher Global Assessment of Functioning (GAF) and Insight scores than others ($R^2 = 0.41$), shown in Table 9.4 and Figure 9.1.

At the end of analysis, the adaptive functioning scores of patients with and without maximum benefits did differ, Wilks' $F(3,45) = 8.44$, $p = 0.0001$. The scores of patients who ended analysis with maximum benefits were higher at the end of analysis than the scores of others: GAF, $F(1,47) = 17.41$, $p = 0.0001$; Insight, $F(1,47) = 12.51$, $p = 0.0009$; and Health, $F(1,47) = 5.80$, $p = 0.02$. On neither the personality disorder nor the trait scale scores did the groups differ overall: Wilks' $F(10, 38) = 1.31$, $p = 0.26$ and Wilks' $F(11, 37) = 0.77$,

Table 9.3 Shedler–Westen Assessment Procedure (SWAP) items at the end of analysis that best describe patients with maximum benefits and others

Item	Mean	SD
With maximum benefits		
183. Is psychologically insightful; is able to understand self and others in subtle and sophisticated ways	6.5	0.8
092. Is articulate; can express self well in words	6.5	0.5
032. Is capable of sustaining a meaningful love relationship characterized by genuine intimacy and caring	6.2	0.8
200. Is able to form close and lasting friendships characterized by mutual support and sharing of experiences	6.2	0.8
089. Appears to have come to terms with painful experiences from the past; has found meaning in, and grown from such experiences	6.0	0.6
019. Enjoys challenges; takes pleasure in accomplishing things	5.8	1.2
120. Has moral and ethical standards and strives to live up to them	5.8	0.8
175. Tends to be conscientious and responsible	5.8	2.9
059. Is empathic; is sensitive and responsive to other people's needs and feelings	5.7	2.8
106. Tends to express affect appropriate in quality and intensity to the situation at hand	5.7	1.0
Others		
092. Is articulate; can express self well in words	4.9	2.4
035. Tends to be anxious	4.8	2.0
068. Appreciates and responds to humor	4.5	2.2
175. Tends to be conscientious and responsible	4.4	2.2
183. Is psychologically insightful; is able to understand self and others in subtle and sophisticated ways	4.3	2.4
120. Has moral and ethical standards and strives to live up to them	4.2	2.0
111. Has the capacity to recognize alternative viewpoints, even in matters that stir up strong feelings	4.1	2.2
091. Tends to be self-critical; sets unrealistically high standards for self and is intolerant of own human defects	4.0	2.1
019. Enjoys challenges; takes pleasure in accomplishing things	3.9	2.5
057. Tends to feel guilty	3.9	2.2
059. Is empathic; is sensitive and responsive to other people's needs and feelings	3.9	2.3
084. Tends to be competitive with others (whether consciously or unconsciously)	3.9	2.2

Table 9.4 Shedler–Westen Assessment Procedure (SWAP) items and SWAP scores at the end of analysis that differentiate between patients with maximum benefits (MB) and others

Predictors of group membership	MB Mean (SD)	Other Mean (SD)	Partial R^2	Model R^2	F	p
Patient factors						
SWAP items						
89. Appears to have come to terms with painful experiences from the past; has found meaning in, and grown from such experiences	6.2 (0.7)	2.5 (2.2)	0.32	0.32	22.46	<0.0001
Personality Disorder Scales						
Paranoid Personality Disorder	34.9 (4.7)	40.7 (8.1)	0.17	0.17	9.36	0.004
Trait Scales						
None are significant						
Adaptive Functioning Scales						
Global Assessment of Functioning	84.9 (14.5)	69.6 (8.7)	0.29	0.29	19.61	<0.0001
Insight	87.7 (6.8)	62.4 (21.1)	0.11	0.41	8.66	0.005

$p = 0.67$ respectively. The SWAP scale and adaptive functioning scores are shown in Figure 9.1.

Analyses

The analyses of patients with maximum benefits from analysis were longer than those of others ($R^2 = 0.22$), as can be seen in Table 9.4. The analyses of the 11 patients whose analyses ended with mutual agreement between patient and analyst and with maximum benefits continued for an average of 62.0 months (SD = 24.9) vs. 28.9 months (SD = 24.8), Wilcoxon $p = 0.0006$ for other patients.

Conclusions

Our goal in this chapter has been to understand more about the characteristics at the beginning of analysis that bode well for an excellent analytic outcome and to understand more about characteristics of people at the end of analysis with maximum benefits. In contrast to other theoretical ideas and empirical findings, scores on psychological health at the beginning of analysis did not differ significantly for those with maximum benefits and others. Perhaps this is because most of the analysands had a reasonable degree of psychological health early in analysis. While the SWAP Psychological Health Scale scores varied (from 47 to 85), the average score was 65.9 (SD = 10.3) and, as a T-score, was 15 points above the average of Westen and Shedler's (1999a, 1999b) normative data on patients in therapy with one of a wide range of personality disorders. An ability to form relationships, hysteria, or insight at the beginning of analysis did not predict maximum benefits. All three features have been proposed in theoretical discussions of who is likely to benefit most from analysis. As has been found in other studies, patients who ended analysis with maximum benefits were in analysis longer than other patients.

On the other hand, as the analyses began, one SWAP item differentiated between the two groups. At the beginning of analysis, patients who would later complete analysis with maximum benefits were viewed as having higher scores than others on the item: "Tends to be overly concerned with rules, procedures, order, organization, schedules, etc." Although the R^2 value, $p = 0.16$, was modest, we think this finding is quite useful. Working out analytic schedules is not a simple matter. At a rather practical level, we are not surprised to realize that this matters.

At the end of analysis, patients who ended analysis with maximum benefits in the view of their analysts had higher scores than others on a single SWAP item, "Appears to have come to terms with painful experiences from the past; has found meaning in, and grown from such experiences," lower scores on the Paranoid Personality Disorder Scale, and higher GAF and Insight scores. An individual SWAP item as well as a SWAP scale score are useful for understanding analyses with maximum benefits.

Before we can fully understand the two groups ending analysis with mutual agreement between analysts and patients with and without maximum benefits, we need to compare these two outcome groups directly. This we will do in the next chapter.

References

Abrams, S. (1992). Psychoanalytic interpretation: A dialogue. *Psychoanalytic Inquiry: A Topical Journal for Mental Health Professionals, 12,* 196–207.

Bachrach, H. M. (1993). The Columbia Records Project and the evolution of psychoanalytic outcome research. *Journal of the American Psychoanalytic Association, 41,* 279–297.

Castonguay, L. G., & Beutler, L. E. (2006). Common and unique principles of therapeutic change: What do we know and what do we need to know. In L. G. Castonguay & L. E. Beutler (Eds.), *Principles of therapeutic change that work.* London: Oxford University Press, pp. 353–369.

Coriat, I. H. (1917). Some statistical results of the psychoanalytic treatment of the psychoneuroses. *Psychoanalytic Review, 4,* 209–216.

Erikson, E. (1950). *Childhood and society.* New York: W. W. Norton. (Reprinted in 1963.)

Fenichel, O. (1945). *The psychoanalytic theory of neurosis.* New York: Norton.

Freud, S. (1895). The psychotherapy of hysteria. In J. Strachey (Ed. and transl.), *The standard edition of the complete psychological works of Sigmund Freud* (Vol. 2). London: Hogarth Press. (Reprinted in 1981.)

Freud, S. (1904). Freud's psychoanalytic procedure. In J. Strachey (Ed. and transl.), *The standard edition of the complete psychological works of Sigmund Freud* (Vol. 7). London: Hogarth Press, pp. 249–254. (Reprinted in 1981.)

Freud, S. (1905). Fragment of an analysis of a case of hysteria. Postscript. In J. Strachey (Ed. and transl.), *The standard edition of the complete psychological works of Sigmund Freud* (Vol. 7). London: Hogarth Press, pp. 1–122. (Reprinted in 1981.)

Freud, S. (1937). Analysis terminable and interminable. In J. Strachey (Ed. and transl.), *The standard edition of the complete psychological works of Sigmund Freud* (Vol. 23). London: Hogarth Press, pp. 211–253. (Reprinted in 1981.)

Glover, E. (1954). Therapeutic criteria of psychoanalysis. *The International Journal of Psychoanalysis, 35*, 95–101.

Jones, E. (1920). *Treatment of the neuroses.* London: Baillière, Tindall and Cox.

Knight, R. P. (1941). Evaluation of the results of psychoanalytic therapy. *American Journal of Psychiatry, 98*, 434–446.

Lower, R. B., Escoll, P. J., & Huxster, H. K. (1972). Bases for judgments of analyzability. *Journal of the American Psychoanalytic Association, 20*, 610–621.

Luborsky, L., & Spence, D. P. (1971). Quantitative research on psychoanalytic therapy. In A. E. Garfield & S. L. Bergin (Eds.), *Handbook of psychotherapy and behavior change: An empirical analysis.* New York: Wiley, pp. 408–438.

Luborsky, L., Auerbach, A. H., Chandler, M., Cohen, J., & Bachrach, H. M. (1971). Factors influencing the outcome of psychotherapy: A review of quantitative research. *Psychological Bulletin, 75*, 145–185.

Luborsky, L., Crits-Christoph, P., Mintz, J., & Auerbach, A. (1988). *Who will benefit from psychotherapy? Predicting therapeutic outcomes.* New York: Basic Books.

Luborsky, L., Diguer, L., Luborsky, E., McLellan, A. T., Woody, G., & Alexander, L. (1993). Psychological health-sickness (PHS) as a predictor of outcomes in dynamic and other psychotherapies. *Journal of Consulting and Clinical Psychology, 61*, 542–548.

Luborsky, L., Docherty, J. P., Miller, N. E., & Barber, J. P. (1993). What's here and what's ahead in dynamic therapy research and practice. *Psychodynamic Treatment Research*, 536–553.

Luborsky, L., Stuart, J., Friedman, S., Diguer, L., Seligman, D. A., Bucci, W., Pulver, S., Krause, E. D., Ermold, J., Daavison, W. T., Woody, G., & Mergenthaler, E. (2001). The Penn Psychoanalytic Treatment Collection: A set of complete and recorded psychoanalyses as a research resource. *Journal of the American Psychoanalytic Association, 49*, 217–234.

Rogers, C. R. (1957). The necessary and sufficient conditions of therapeutic personality change. *Journal of Consulting Psychology, 21*, 95–103.

Sandler, J., Holder, A., & Dare, C. (1970). Basic psychoanalytic concepts: VII. The negative therapeutic reaction. *British Journal of Psychiatry, 117*, 431–435.

Schofield, W. (1964). *Psychotherapy: The purchase of friendship.* Englewood Cliffs, NJ: Prentice Hall.

Shedler, J. (2010). The efficacy of psychodynamic psychotherapy. *American Psychologist, 65(2)*, 98–109.

Tolstoy, L. (1954). *Anna Karenina.* (R. Edmonds, transl.) New York: Penguin. (Translation reprinted 1978.)

Weber, J. J., Bachrach, H. M., & Solomon, M. (1985). Factors associated with the outcome of psychoanalysis: Report of the Columbia Psychoanalytic Center research project (III). *International Review of Psychoanalysis, 12*, 251–262.

Westen, D., & Shedler, J. (1999a). Revising and assessing Axis II, Part I: Developing a clinically and empirically valid assessment method. *American Journal of Psychiatry, 156(2)*, 258–272.

Westen, D., & Shedler, J. (1999b). Revising and assessing Axis II, Part II: Toward an empirically based and clinically useful classification of personality disorders. *American Journal of Psychiatry, 156(2)*, 273–285.

Wolpe, J. (1958). *Psychotherapy by reciprocal inhibition.* Standford: Stanford University Press.

Zetzel, E. R. (1965). The theory of therapy in relation to a developmental model of the psychic apparatus. *International Journal of Psychoanalysis, 46*, 39–52.

Chapter 10

Analyses ending with mutual agreement between patient and analyst

With vs. without maximum benefits

> They [self-actualized people] are the most ethical of people even though their ethics are not necessarily the same as those of the people around them.
>
> (Maslow, 1950a)

Introduction

In case presentations in conferences or in courses on the termination of analysis in psychoanalytic institutes, it is not unusual to hear the treating analyst or someone else differentiate between analyses ending with maximum benefits and analyses ending with positive outcomes but with reservations as to how complete or truly effective the analysis really was. For instance, the analyst might say of the patient, "They did well but I think they could have used more analysis." Empirical studies of the outcome of psychoanalysis often differentiate between patients who are "cured," are "much improved," or 'have maximum benefits" and patients who are simply "improved." However, statements like these are often puzzling because they are rarely followed by a description of exactly what the differences were between the various outcomes. Unfortunately there seem to be no empirical data that makes it clear exactly what differentiates between analyses ending with and analyses ending without maximum benefits.

In Chapter 8, we considered analyses ending without maximum benefits as compared with the other analyses in the longitudinal project. In Chapter 9, we considered analyses ending with maximum benefits as compared with the other analyses in the longitudinal project. We will now directly compare the analyses of patients who ended analysis with and patients who ended analysis without maximum benefits in the longitudinal study. Both of these groups ended analysis with mutual agreement between analyst and patient; both had positive changes. What characteristics at the beginning of analysis predict the two outcomes and how are the two groups different at the end of analysis?

As the analyses began

Patients

The Shedler–Westen Assessment Procedure (SWAP) items most characteristic of patients in the two groups at the beginning of analysis are shown in Table 10.1. People in both groups were described as having moral and ethical standards, being conscientious, articulate, and self-critical, and feeling guilty. Beyond this, the pictures are quite different. As the analyses began, people who ended analysis with maximum benefit were described as being empathic, likeable, and able to form lasting friendships, but also as anxious and having problems expressing anger. That is, their more problematic features involved affects and enough of their difficulties with anxiety and with expressing anger had come into the analytic conversation to be identified as salient by the analyst. People who ended analysis without maximum benefits were described with positive features including finding meaning in belonging to a larger community, being insightful, and as responding to humor. They were also described as being easily influenced and inhibited about pursuing goals. The less than positive features of patients who ended analysis without maximum benefits could well be problematic with respect to reaching maximum benefits in psychoanalysis.

Four SWAP items early in analysis predicted group membership in a stepwise regression analysis of SWAP-200 items of patients with and without maximum benefits. As the analyses began, patients who ended analysis with maximum benefits were seen as more able to find satisfaction in pursuing long-term goals (mean (M)= 4.6) as compared to patients who ended analysis without maximum benefits ($M = 1.7$; $R^2 = 0.43$). Patients whose analyses ended with maximum benefits also had less trouble focusing on details and were seen as somewhat more hostile and more ashamed or embarrassed than people who ended analysis without maximum benefits. The overall $R^2 = 0.91$, shown in Table 10.2. The items are poignant in the context of completing analysis with maximum benefits, which surely demands an ability to move toward long-term goals and an ability to focus on details. Perhaps being experienced as the analysis began as somewhat more angry and ashamed – which, while not extreme, were more characteristic of patients ending analysis with than patients ending analysis without maximum benefits – has to do with the relative ability to experience and express problematic affects which may, perhaps, facilitate the work of analysis.

In stepwise regression analyses, the SWAP Adaptive Functioning, Personality Disorder and Trait Scale scores did not differentiate between the two groups as the analyses began.

Direct comparisons of the scale scores of patients in the two groups as the analyses began yielded no significant overall differences in the SWAP Personality Disorder Scale scores, the SWAP Trait Scale scores, or the adaptive

Table 10.1 Shedler–Westen Assessment Procedure (SWAP) items at the beginning of analysis that best describe patients who finished with and without maximum benefits

Item	Mean	SD
With maximum benefits		
120. Has moral and ethical standards and strives to live up to them	5.8	1.1
175. Tends to be conscientious and responsible	5.8	2.0
092. Is articulate; can express self well in words	5.7	1.3
059. Is empathic; is sensitive and responsive to other people's needs and feelings	5.5	1.9
091. Tends to be self-critical; sets unrealistically high standards for self and is intolerant of own human defects	5.5	1.9
051. Tends to elicit liking in others	5.4	1.5
057. Tends to feel guilty	5.3	2.0
025. Has difficulty acknowledging or expressing anger	5.2	1.2
035. Tends to be anxious	5.2	1.9
200. Is able to form close and lasting friendships characterized by mutual support and sharing of experiences	5.0	1.9
Without maximum benefits		
037. Finds meaning in belong and contributing to a larger community (e.g., organization, church, neighborhood, etc.)	5.0	1.4
120. Has moral and ethical standards and strives to live up to them	4.8	1.2
046. Tends to be suggestible or easily influenced	4.7	1.4
033. Appears inhibited about pursuing goals or successes; aspirations or achievements tend to be below his/her potential	4.3	3.4
057. Tends to feel guilty	4.3	2.4
068. Appreciates and responds to humor	4.2	2.9
092. Is articulate; can express self well in words.	4.2	2.2
091. Tends to be self-critical; sets unrealistically high standards for self and is intolerant of own human defects	4.0	2.0
175. Tends to be conscientious and responsible	4.0	2.6
183. Is psychologically insightful; is able to understand self and others in subtle and sophisticated ways	4.0	2.1

functioning scores of the two groups, Wilks' $F(10,6) = 2.43$, $p = 0.05$, Wilks' $F(11,5) = 1.35$, $p = 0.39$, and Wilks' $F(3,12) = 0.87$, $p = 0.48$ respectively, shown in Figure 10.1.

The two groups did not differ in sex, age, race, marital status, socioeconomic status, education, number of Axis I or Axis II clinical diagnoses, taking psychotropic medications, having alcohol or drug problems, or having had previous mental health treatment. Wilcoxon p ranged from 0.08 to 0.91.

Table 10.2 Shedler–Westen Assessment Procedure (SWAP) items, and scale scores at the beginning of analysis that differentiate between patients with and without maximum benefits (MB)

Predictors of group membership	With MB Mean (SD)	Without MB Mean (SD)	r	R^2	F	p
SWAP items						
196. Is able to find meaning and satisfaction in the pursuit of long-term goals and ambitions	4.6 (1.9)	1.7 (1.5)	0.43	0.43	11.19	0.004
072. Perceptions seem glib, global, and impressionistic; has difficulty focusing on specific details	0.2 (0.6)	1.0 (0.9)	0.24	0.67	9.96	0.007
016. Tends to be angry or hostile (whether consciously or unconsciously)	2.5 (2.2)	1.5 (1.4)	0.15	0.82	10.64	0.006
086. Tends to feel ashamed or embarrassed	3.9 (0.7)	3.0 (2.0)	0.09	0.91	12.65	0.004
Personality Disorder Scales						
None are significant						
Trait Scales						
None are significant						
Adaptive Functioning Scales						
None are significant						

Analysts

The analysts in the two groups did not differ in sex, profession, years of professional experience, years of psychoanalytic experience, or their endorsement of primary theoretical orientations. Wilcoxon p ranged from 0.10 to 0.34.

Analyses

The two groups differed somewhat in the use of the couch as analysis began, Wilcoxon $p = 0.03$ (slightly above the required adjusted p value of 0.02). While all of the 11 patients whose analyses ended with maximum benefits were on the couch as the analyses began, two of the six patients whose analyses ended without maximum benefits were not on the couch and one was not on the couch consistently as the analyses began. The two groups did not differ in the frequency of analytic sessions, Wilcoxon $p = 0.27$, or the fee, Wilcoxon $p = 0.39$.

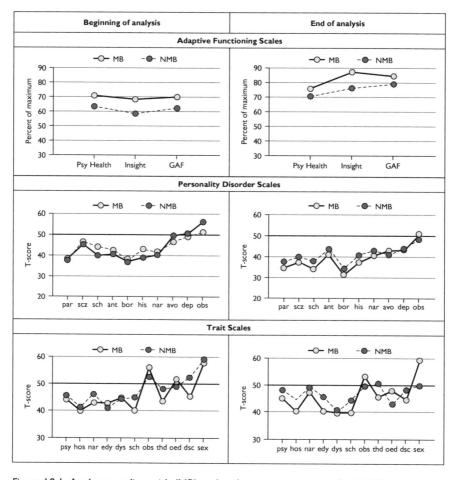

Figure 10.1 Analyses ending with (MB) and without maximum benefits (NMB) at the beginning and end of analysis

Adaptive Functioning Scales: Psychological Health, Insight, Global Assessment of Functioning (GAF).

Personality Disorder Scales: Paranoid, Schizoid, Schizotypal, Antisocial, Borderline, Histrionic, Narcissistic, Avoidant, Dependent, and Obsessive.

Trait Scales: Psychopathy, Hostility, Narcissism, Emotional Dysregulation, Dysphoria, Schizoid Orientation, Obsessionality, Thought Disorder, Oedipal Conflict, Dissociation, and Sexual Conflict.

At the end of analysis

At the end of analysis, people in both groups were described as insightful, empathic, able to sustain both love relationships and close friendships, enjoying challenges, and having come to terms with painful experiences from the past,

Table 10.3 Shedler–Westen Assessment Procedure (SWAP) items at the end of analysis that best describe patients who finished with and without maximum benefits

Item	Mean	SD
With maximum benefits		
092. Is articulate; can express self well in words	6.6	0.5
183. Is psychologically insightful; is able to understand self and others in subtle and sophisticated ways	6.5	0.8
120. Has moral and ethical standards and strives to live up to them	6.4	0.9
032. Is capable of sustaining a meaningful love relationship characterized by genuine intimacy and caring	6.2	0.8
089. Appears to have come to terms with painful experiences from the past; has found meaning in, and grown from such experiences	6.2	0.7
175. Tends to be conscientious and responsible	6.1	2.5
200. Is able to form close and lasting friendships characterized by mutual support and sharing of experiences	6.1	0.6
121. Is creative; is able to see things or approach problems in novel ways	5.9	0.8
019. Enjoys challenges; takes pleasure in accomplishing things	5.8	1.2
059. Is empathic; is sensitive and responsive to other people's needs and feelings	5.8	2.4
Without maximum benefits		
019. Enjoys challenges; takes pleasure in accomplishing things	6.2	1.6
032. Is capable of sustaining a meaningful love relationship characterized by genuine intimacy and sharing	6.0	0.8
037. Finds meaning in belonging and contributing to a larger community (e.g., organization, church, neighborhood, etc.)	6.0	2.0
200. Is able to form close and lasting friendships characterized by mutual support and sharing of experiences	5.8	1.5
068. Appreciates and responds to humor	5.5	0.7
089. Appears to have come to terms with painful experiences from the past; has found meaning in, and grown from such experiences	5.5	1.4
002. Is able to use his/her talents, abilities, and energy effectively and productively	5.3	1.6
063. Is able to assert him/herself effectively and appropriately when necessary	5.2	0.8
183. Is psychologically insightful; is able to understand self and others in subtle and sophisticated ways	5.2	2.2
059. Is empathic; is sensitive and responsive to other people's needs and feelings	5.0	1.8

shown in Table 10.3. People who ended analysis without maximum benefit were described as able to use their talents productively, and as able to assert themselves appropriately; they were described as finding meaning in belonging to a larger community and as responding to humor. People who ended analysis with maximum benefits were described as being conscientious and responsible, having moral and ethical standards, and as creative and articulate.

Three SWAP items differentiated between the two groups at the end of analysis in a stepwise regression analysis. As the analyses ended, patients who ended analysis with maximum benefits were more characterized as having moral and ethical standards and striving to live up to them ($M = 6.4$) as compared to patients who ended analysis without maximum benefits ($M = 4.3$; $R^2 = 0.66$). As the analyses ended, patients who ended analysis with maximum benefits were seen as somewhat more likely to find sexual experiences as slightly revolting or disgusting, and as more conscientious and responsible than patients who ended analysis without maximum benefits. The overall $R^2 = 0.94$, shown in Table 10.4.

Direct comparisons of the scale scores of patients in the two groups as the analyses ended yielded no significant overall differences in the Personality Disorder Scale scores, Wilks' $F(10,4) = 1.96$, $p = 0.37$; trait scale scores, Wilks' $F(11,3) = 1.33$, $p = 0.46$ or adaptive functioning scale scores, Wilks' $F(3,11) = 1.40, p = 0.29$.

Table 10.4 Shedler–Westen Assessment Procedure (SWAP) items, and scale scores at the end of analysis that differentiate between patients with and without maximum benefits (MB)

Predictors of group membership	With MB Mean (SD)	Without MB Mean (SD)	r	R^2	F	p
SWAP items						
120. Has moral and ethical standards and strives to live up to them	6.4 (0.9)	4.3 (0.5)	0.66	0.66	23.70	0.004
118. Tends to see sexual experiences as revolting or disgusting	0.5 (1.1)	0.0 (0.0)	0.19	0.85	14.08	0.003
175. Tends to be conscientious and responsible	6.1 (2.5)	3.7 (1.2)	0.09	0.94	15.43	0.003
Personality Disorder Scales						
None are significant						
Trait Scales						
None are significant						
Adaptive Functioning Scales						
None are significant						

Analyses

As the analyses ended, the two groups did not differ in the setting, frequency, use of the couch, or fee. Wilcoxon *p* ranged from 0.11 to 0.95. Although the analyses ending with maximum benefits were longer than those ending without maximum benefits ($M = 62.0$ months, SD $= 24.9$ months vs. $M = 55.2$ months, SD $= 23.0$), the difference did not approach statistical significance, Wilcoxon $p = 0.23$.

Conclusions

When we began this set of three chapters focused on people ending analysis with mutual agreement between patients and analysts, we reviewed the ideas in the theoretical and clinical literature about characteristics of people for whom analysis was most effective. An ability to form relationships, hysteria, and psychological mindedness were characteristics associated with analyzability in the theoretical literature. Much to our surprise, however, none of these came into the characteristics differentiating people with and without maximum benefits. However, we then went back to the SWAP scale scores and SWAP items that best described all of the patients at the beginning of analysis in Chapter 3. The analysands as a group were not high on the Histrionic Personality Disorder Scale; nor were they troubled as a group with high scores on the Thought Disorder Scale, the Emotional Dysregulation Scale, or the Paranoid Personality Disorder Scale. However, the analysands as a group were higher on SWAP Psychological Health Scale and Insight Scale scores than was characteristic of the patient population for which the scales were originally normed (Lehmann, 2012; Westen & Shedler, 1999). We found as well that the analysands as a group were described as empathic, likeable, and able to recognize alternative viewpoints. The exception was the three analysands whose analyses ended with a negative therapeutic reaction. It seems likely that, as the analyses began, with the exception of analysands whose analyses ended with a negative therapeutic reaction, the analysands actually did have much in common with the classical ideas about who would benefit from psychoanalysis.

At the beginning of analysis, people whose analyses ended with maximum benefits were able to find meaning in pursuing long-term goals. Persisting in analysis understandably requires planning and an ability to pursue long-term goals. They were also able to be aware of and express painful affects such as anger. As analysis began, each of the 11 patients who ended analysis with maximum benefits and only three of the six who ended without maximum benefits were consistently on the couch. At the beginning of analysis, perhaps those who eventually ended analysis without maximum benefit were less comfortable using the couch and free associating and needed the comfort and support of being able to see their analyst.

At the end of analysis, people whose analyses ended with maximum benefits were characterized as having and trying to live up to moral and ethical standards. They also had slightly higher scores on seeing sexual experiences in a negative light. This may suggest a greater capacity to be aware of and express feelings about sexual experiences or may suggest new ideas about sexual experiences. Finally, they were conscientious and responsible, characteristics that would have served to support analytic work.

Although our conclusions should be taken with caution because of the small number of subjects, we think the data shed light on early psychoanalytic conversations about ethical issues and treatment goals. We are reminded by Blass (2003) about letters from Freud to Putman in 1914: The aim of treatment, Freud wrote, is to bring about "the highest ethical and intellectual development of the individual" (p. 939). Maslow (1950b) has described people who are self-actualized as "the most ethical of people." Neither Freud nor anyone else is proposing ideal moral virtue at the end of analysis with maximum benefits. We do think, however, that the present findings indicate that having moral and ethical standards and trying to live up to them, and all that this entails about life, has an important role in analysts' views of what people are like at the end of analyses with maximum benefits. At a structural level, this may have to do with superego development. Perhaps most centrally, the findings support a differentiation of analyses ending with mutual agreement between analyst and patient with and without maximum benefits.

References

Blass, R. B. (2003). On ethical issues at the foundation of the debate over the goals of psychoanalysis. *International Journal of Psychoanalysis, 84,* 929–943.

Lehmann, M. E. (2012). Evaluating pre-treatment patient insight as a factor in early therapeutic technique. Unpublished doctoral dissertation, Adelphi University.

Maslow, A. H. (1950a). *Towards a psychology of being.* New York: Wiley.

Maslow, A. H. (1950b). Self-actualizing people: A study of psychological health. *Personality,* Symposium No. 1, 11–34.

Westen, D., & Shedler, J. (1999). Revising and assessing Axis II, Part I: Developing a clinically and empirically valid assessment method. *American Journal of Psychiatry, 156(2),* 258–272.

Part III

Insight and change

Chapter 11

The role of insight in change with N. G. Cogan

Psychoanalysis is not without a goal,
but has the inexorable goal of expanded insight.

(Blum, 1979)

Introduction

Consideration of insight has a long history, going back to the words "Know Thyself," inscribed on the entryway to the Temple of Delphi. Perhaps insight has a profound role in promoting change in psychoanalysis. Perhaps most readers believe this to be true and perhaps the only debate might be whether interpretation or the relationship between the patient and analyst is the central mechanism that promotes insight. We confess immediately that we have no evidence to bear on the question about the mechanisms that promote insight. What we can contribute to the discussion has to do with the relationship between insight and change in psychoanalysis.

As others have noted (cf. Sandler, Dare, & Holder, 1973), the word "insight" is not in the index of *The Collected Works of Sigmund Freud*. This is all the more interesting given that thinking about insight was central to the development of psychoanalysis (Blum, 1979; Crits-Christoph, Barber, Miller, & Beebe, 1993; Fisher & Greenberg, 1977; Kris, 1956; Reid & Finesinger, 1952; Sandler et al., 1973; Zilboorg, 1952). As Freud was developing the theory and technique of psychoanalysis, consideration of insight was active in the wider intellectual world. In Germany, the gestalt thinkers Kohler, Koffka, and Wertheimer were considering insight in a different context (Ash, 1998). Kohler observed and wrote about the sudden "a-ha" changes in the behavior of primates unable to reach food they wanted and then very abruptly putting two sticks together and collecting the food with the joined sticks (e.g., Kohler, 1925/1959). In Russia, Pavlov knew and wrote of Freud's work with Anna O., which related to Pavlov's study of types of dogs in 1910 and of his studies of experimental neuroses in dogs (cf. Todes, 2014). Film footage from a nursery in Pavlov's lab where he studied children shows something similar as a child very suddenly puts a chair on top of a table so that he can reach a kind of toy hanging out of reach on the wall. Thinking about insight certainly became part of the zeitgeist. Discussions of insight are pervasive in all types of contemporary psychotherapies, including cognitive-behavioral therapy (cf. Grosse Holtforth, Castonguay, Boswell, Kakouros, & Borkevec, 2007).

Studies of insight

Measures

Measures of insight in clinical situations vary considerably and no one measure has been widely or consistently adopted. Measures have been based on patients' story completions (e.g., Sargent, 1944, 1953), and on patients' understanding of the dynamics of patient–therapist interactions by actors shown in videotapes (McCallum & Piper, 1990; McCullough et al., 2004) or transcripts (Hohage & Kubler, 1988). Self-report measures completed by patients have been developed (e.g., Beck, Baruch, Balter, Steer, & Warman, 2004; Birchwood, Smith, Drury, Healy, & Slad, 1994; Grossman, 1951). Other measures have involved ratings of patients' insights from transcripts of psychotherapy sessions or interviews or case summaries (Hohage & Kubler, 1988; Kivlighan, Multon, & Patton, 2000; Sandell, 1987). Measures have included the treating clinician's ratings of the patient's insight (Gelso, Kivlighan, Wine, Jones, & Friedman, 1997). The recently developed Shedler–Westen Assessment Procedure (SWAP) Insight Scale, a clinician report measure (Lehman & Hilsenroth, 2011), will be described below.

Changes in insight during psychotherapy and psychoanalysis

Low insight at the beginning of individual therapy has been related to dropping out of psychotherapy (McCallum & Piper, 1990). Increases in insight have been reported during dynamic psychotherapy (Cromer & Hilsenroth, 2010; Hoglend, Engelstad, Sorbye, Heyerdahl, & Amlo, 1994; Johansson et al., 2010; Jones, Parke, & Pulos, 1992; Kivlighan et al., 2000; O'Connor, Edelstein, Berry, & Weiss, 1994; Rosenbaum, Friedlander, & Kaplan, 1956; Sandell, 1987), but not during brief interventions (Diemer, Lobell, Vivino, & Hill, 1996) or short-term treatments of 12 sessions or less, whether group, cognitive, or psychodynamic therapy (Ablon & Jones, 1999; Gelso, Kivlighan, Wine, Jones, & Friedman, 1997; Kallestad et al., 2010; McCallum & Piper, 1990). Increases in insight have been related to more positive therapy outcomes (Ablon & Jones, 1999; Connolly et al., 1999; Gelso et al., 1997; Grande, Rudolf, Oberbracht, & Pauli-Magnus, 2003; Hoglend et al., 1994; Johansson et al., 2010; Jones et al., 1992; Kallestad et al., 2010; Kivlighan et al., 2000).

Only a few studies have considered changes in insight over the course of therapy. Over sessions, decreases followed by increases in insight have been reported in six very short-term cases of psychotherapy (Raskin, 1949), four cases of 16-session psychotherapy (O'Connor et al., 1994), and 12 20-session cases of psychodynamic psychotherapy (Kivlighan et al., 2000). Studying changes in insight over the course of psychoanalysis will provide new information about the role of insight in changes in personality and symptoms.

Further, psychoanalysis is generally considered to have a beginning, middle, and termination phase (e.g., Fenichel, 1941; Greenson, 1967). Freud commented (1913/1981):

> Anyone who hopes to learn the noble game of chess from books will soon discover that only the openings and end-games admit of an exhaustive systematic presentation and that the infinite variety of moves which develop after the opening defy any such description. The gap in instruction can only be filled by a diligent study of games fought out by masters. The rules which can be laid down for the practice of psycho-analytic treatment are subject to similar limitations.
>
> (p. 123)

Studying changes in insight during psychoanalysis may also help shed light on phases of analysis.

The present cases

Up to this point in this longitudinal study, we have compared differences between groups as analyses began and as they ended. Here we will consider changes in insight over the course of psychoanalysis in patients who completed psychoanalysis with maximum benefits.[1] We will then consider the relationship between changes in SWAP Insight Scale scores and in Psychological Health, Paranoid Personality Disorder, and Dysphoria Trait Scale scores. The reason for the choice of these scales is described below. Finally, we will consider identification of the three phases of psychoanalysis.

Method

The analyses of the nine patients with maximum benefits and SWAP data over the course of analysis continued for an average of 59.3 months (SD = 27.0 months). Insight began at 30.2 (SD = 13.2) of the possible 42 points on the SWAP Insight Scale and ended at 36.9 (SD = 6.8) of the possible 42 points on the scale.[2]

We chose one scale from each of the three domains of the SWAP scores to include here. We chose Psychological Health as an adaptive functioning scale. We chose the Paranoid Personality Disorder Scale because it showed marked range in our five outcome groups and differentiated significantly between patients ending with maximum benefits and other patients. It is not an especially high scale at the beginning of psychoanalysis among patients whose analyses ended with maximum benefits, but allowed us to explore the possibility of dynamic changes in one of the Personality Disorder Scales. Finally, we chose the Dysphoria Trait Scale because it was relatively high among the Trait Scales and because we expected that dysphoria, which "measures chronic feelings of depression, inadequacy, meaningless, emptiness, and shame" (Shedler, 2009), would have meaning for all readers.

In this chapter we turn to mathematical modeling to help explain and quantify the relationship between changes in Insight and changes in the other three dimensions. There are three immediate goals of the mathematical modeling described below. First, since the length of time of the psychoanalyses varied widely, we develop a method of adjusting the data so that we can compare psychoanalyses that vary in length. Second, we will use mathematics to help identify the beginning, middle, and end phases of psychoanalysis. Finally, we will explore the relationship between changes in Insight and changes in our three other dimensions.

Mathematicians typically develop models in two different ways. They may begin with a bottom-up approach, which uses generally agreed-upon physical laws to describe a set of experiments or observations using algebraic (essentially static), differential (typically dynamic in time, but not space), or partial differential (dynamic in multiple dimensions such as time and physical space) equations. For the bottom-up approach many parameters may need to be estimated, but an honest modeler will do the smallest possible amount of tuning. There is a colloquial saying in modeling that "given enough parameters, my model can fit an elephant." Another difficulty with the bottom-up approach that is apparent in modeling biological processes, and is felt even more keenly in psychological applications, is that there are no universal laws that can be relied upon. In physics, there are no serious arguments about the law of conservation of mass. Even Newton's laws are not seriously questioned until one reaches speeds approaching the speed of light, or sizes approaching the quantum level. In this regard, psychoanalytic modeling is clearly in its preliminary stage.

In contrast to the bottom-up approach, a modeler may take a top-down approach. Here, mathematicians rely on the data, ideas of people working in the area, historically useful models, and a series of assumptions to develop a model that seems predictive of the particular case in point. This model may be used to make predictions that were not evident and may be tested quantitatively as predictions or postdictions to fit a wider set of data than was used to formulate the model. Often these types of models have more specific applications than bottom-up models but the process of formulating the model helps clarify key assumptions, time-scales, and differences between data sets. Even though these models are not easily translated to other loosely related topics, they can provide information not readily available through observational studies. The mathematical analysis in this chapter is squarely in the top-down approach and we will try to be quite clear about our assumptions and predictions.

Interpolating the data

The first difficulty that we encounter in the study data is that the time in analysis varied from 28 to 121 months for the analyses with maximum benefits. It seems reasonable, especially in light of the idea that there may be phases of analysis, to assume that, while some patients finish analysis more quickly than others, they each pass through similar stages. Therefore we decided to scale time, t for each sample by the total time in analysis, T. The new, dimensionless time variable $\tau = \dfrac{t}{T}$, now lies in the interval [0,1] for all samples. We interpolate the data on to regularly spaced intervals, making comparisons straight-forward.

After this transformation of the time variable, we see a distinct inter-relationship between Insight and Dysphoria. After an initial period of transient dynamics, Dysphoria and Insight were both oscillating, but out of phase until towards the end of analysis. The Paranoia and Psychological Health scores were not as dynamic with respect to varying Insight and apparently followed Insight dynamics, providing a path towards a simple top-down model. The changes over analysis are shown in Figure 11.1.

With these observations, we can develop models for the beginning, middle, and termination phases and can try and understand the relative length of each phase. We assume that the most complicated dynamics occur in the middle phase of analysis and that Insight and Dysphoria are coupled while Insight drives both Psychological Health and Paranoia. Mathematically that means that Insight and Dysphoria are coupled equations while changes in Psychological Health and Paranoia depend on Insight, but not vice versa.

Developing the model

We now describe the mathematical model for each of the phases of analysis. We define the variables $I(t)$, $D(t)$, $P(t)$, $H(t)$, for Insight, Dyspohoria, Paranoia, and Psychological Health Scale scores respectively. We assume that the dynamics of Insight and Dysphoria depend on both Dysphoria and Insight while the dynamics of P and H depend only on Insight and P (or H). This leads to a system of differential equations:

$$\frac{dI}{dt} = f_1(I, D), \tag{1}$$

$$\frac{dD}{dt} = f_2(I, D), \tag{2}$$

$$\frac{dH}{dt} = f_3(I, H), \tag{3}$$

$$\frac{dP}{dt} = f_4(I, P). \tag{4}$$

The functions f_1, f_2, f_3, f_4 define the dynamics – that is, the right-hand sides define the rate at which the state (or dynamic) variables change.

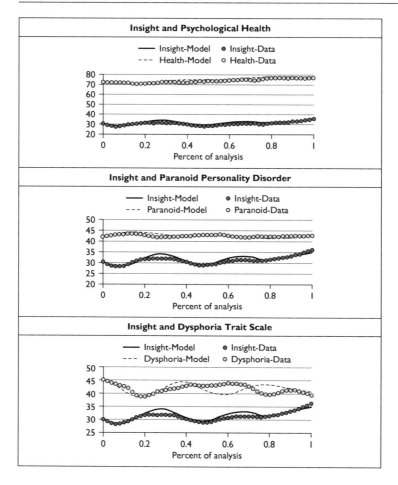

Figure 11.1 Changes in Insight and Psychological Health, Paranoid Personality Disorder, and Dysphoria Scale scores during analysis ending with maximum benefits

Adaptive Functioning Scales: Psychological Health (*r*-factor score), Insight (raw score).

Personality Disorder Scale: Paranoid (*r*-factor score).

Trait Scale: Dysphoria (*r*-factor score).

In calculus, we learn that the derivative (rate of change) of position describes the velocity, so in some sense differential equations link the rate of change of a variable to the particular state of the variable. This is the key insight that Newton introduced that allowed the flexibility to apply calculus to an incredible array of problems.

To specify the solution to the differential equations, we also must define initial conditions which we take from the initial observational data, so that:

$$I(0) \ = I_0$$

$$D(0) = D_0$$

$$H(0) = H_0$$

$$P(0) = P_0$$

To develop the model, we make the assumption that in the initial stages I, D, H and P are essentially independent, with I, D, and H decreasing while P is increasing. At time T_1, the dynamics alter and Paranoia and Psychological Health are both increasing at a constant rate and are influenced by Insight. If Insight increases past a threshold value, Psychological Health increases while Paranoia decreases; below that threshold the opposite is true. This is an example of a mathematical assumption that reflects the data, even though we may have no specific reason to believe or disbelieve the form of the assumption.

At the same time the Dysphoria and Insight dynamics are coupled. Insight alone is increasing at a rate proportional to itself, while Dysphoria decreases similarly – implying that these are exponentially increasing (Insight) and decreasing functions (Dysphoria) if one could separate them. The coupling introduces non-linearities where the interaction between Insight and Dysphoria suppresses Insight and increases Dysphoria.

This is a classic predator/prey interaction that refers to a well-studied class of differential equations developed independently by Lotka and Volterra in the early 1900s (Edelstein-Keshet, 1988). Volterra derived the equations to describe the coupling between a predator population (sharks) and a prey population (sardines). In the midst of World War I, sardine fishing was drastically reduced. It seemed intuitive that when fishing resumed there would be ample prey fish; however, the opposite was true – there was an over-abundance of predator fish. This was followed by oscillations in the fish population. The model that Volterra developed was similar to one that Lotka used to describe a specific chemical reaction. Volterra (1928) argued that, in the absence of predators, the prey fish would grow without bounds (clearly not physically realistic, but simple to study mathematically), while the predators would decay in the absence of prey (also simplistic, since predator fish can actually consume a host of prey, but again mathematically tractable). Whenever a predator and a prey encountered one another, the prey would lose (meaning a decrease in the prey population) and the predator would win (meaning an increase in the predator population). It is quite simple to show that there are only two time-independent solutions (steady states). One is trivial, where the prey are consumed to extinction, followed by the predator, and another where the prey are kept in check by the predators, but reproduce fast enough to allow the predators a constant food source.

Interestingly, for a wide range of parameters, neither steady state is stable. Instead there exists a periodic solution with the predator/prey populations oscillating in time, but out of phase. As the predators increase, the prey decrease, limiting the predator population growth. This leads to a decline in the predator population, allowing the prey population to increase. By analogy, we assume that increasing Insight leads to decreasing Dysphoria. Similarly, Dysphoria can delay the change in Insight that would be expected while in analysis. Given the correspondence to the Lotka–Volterra equation, we expect that, for a wide range of parameters, Dysphoria and Insight will oscillate out of phase. In an analogous manner, it is often customary to assume some saturation in the growth of one of the dependent variables to stabilize the non-trivial equilibria – physically this is just assuming that one or both of the variables is not allowed to grow without bounds in the absence of the other variable. In Lotka–Volterra models, this is typically assumed for the prey species. Here we require a similar restriction for Insight.

Since we assume that the dynamics of Paranoia and Psychological Health depend explicitly on Insight, we make a reasonable assumption that, during the main or middle phase of analysis, Psychological Health increases if Insight is above a threshold while Paranoia decreases if Insight is high enough. In the termination phase of analysis, we note that the data show that Psychological Health and Paranoia change slowly, while Insight tends to increase and Dysphoria decreases. This sort of heuristic assumption allows us to formulate a model that is consistent with the data.

We can incorporate these statements into our mathematical model through our definitions of the right-hand sides of Equations 1–4. Since we are assuming that there are changes in the dynamics at specific times, T_1 and T_2, the functions will be defined piecewise:

$$f_1(t) = \begin{cases} -p_1\, I(t) \text{ if } 0 \leq T_1, \\ p_2 I(t)\left(1 - \dfrac{I(t)}{p_3}\right) + p_4 I(t)\, D(t) \text{ if } T_1 < t \leq T_2, \\ p_5\, I(\text{t}) \text{ if } T_2 < t \leq 1, \end{cases}$$

$$f_2(t) = \begin{cases} -q_1 D(t) \text{ if } 0 \leq T_1, \\ -q_2 D(t) - q_3 I(t) D(t) \text{ if } T_1 < t \leq T_2, \\ -q_4 D(t) \text{ if } T_2 < t \leq 1. \end{cases}$$

$$f_3(t) = \begin{cases} -r_1 H\,(t) \text{ if } 0 \leq T_1, \\ r_2 (I(t) - \hat{I}) \text{ if } T_1 < t \leq T_2, \\ r_3 H\,(t) \text{ if } T_2 < t \leq 1, \end{cases}$$

$$f_4(t) = \begin{cases} s_1 P(t) \text{ if } 0 \leq T_1, \\ -s_2 (I(t) - \hat{I}) \text{ if } T_1 < t \leq T_2, \\ s_3 P(t) \text{ if } T_2 < t \leq 1, \end{cases}$$

where p_*, q_*, r_* and s_* denote parameters for each of the dynamics. In practice it is normal to non-dimensionalize the equations to reduce the number of parameters, but in this case the non-dimensionalization does not reduce the parameter space very much. We also note that, because the right-hand side functions depend explicitly on time, this is formally a system of non-autonomous differential equations, but since the dependence is only piecewise, we can actually analyze the behavior both analytically and in the phase plane.

For now it is enough to note the qualitative behavior for each phase.

- During the early, transient phase the solutions are exponential (either increasing or decreasing, depending on the sign of the leading parameter).
- In the middle phase, there is a decoupled system of dynamics for the (I,D) behavior which has two equilibria – the origin, which is unstable, and a non-trivial, stable equilibrium. Simple linearization indicates that the eigenvalues of the Jacobian matrix are complex (with negative real parts), which implies that the approach to the equilibria occurs with oscillations. Because Insight is oscillating, if we define the reference value $\hat{I}$ to be the stable equilibria for the Insight variable, we see that both Psychological Health and Paranoia oscillate around the midline.
- In the final stage, Insight steadily increases, Dysphoria decreases, and Psychological Health increases while Paranoia decreases.

From this model, we have already been able to make certain observations – some are more qualitative than others. Of course this comes with the caveat that there are likely to be other models that also fit the data and without more exploration, this model can only serve as an outline of the behavior. For example, it seems evident from the data that there is quantitative support for the argument that psychoanalysis can be divided into three phases. In fact, the model helps estimate the percentage of time in analysis spent in each of the phases by using T_1 and T_2 as parameters to fit the model to the data. From our rough estimates, the beginning phase of analysis is quite short (approximately 10% of the time in analysis) while approximately 25% of the time in analysis is spent in the termination phase.

A second observation tied to our model concerns the role of Insight and change. In classic predator/prey modeling, where there are oscillations of two populations that are out of phase, it is customary to talk about "which one moves first?" Mathematically this is not a well-formulated question, since the assumption is that they move together, but in opposing directions. However, to interpret the curves one could reasonably say that Insight leads the change, especially in the transition between the beginning and middle phases of psychoanalysis. One can argue that the model is showing that Insight rises first, altering the Dysphoria, since Insight is playing the role of the prey species in Lotka–Volterra terms, and is in some sense the underlying variable.

The model described above is by no means definitive. It is highly unlikely that our top-down approach describes any absolute relationships between the measures. However, the process of developing a temporary model that describes certain aspects of the data can help frame future questions as well as estimate quantifiable relationships. For the latter, the model indicates that there is support for delineating analysis into three stages. Moreover, the model analysis indicates that the initial phase is much shorter than the middle or last phase and that the last phase is surprisingly long relative to the time in analysis. Additionally, our preliminary efforts indicate that there is support for viewing Insight as the underlying variable that, in some sense, governs the dynamics of psychoanalysis.

Even more importantly, from the scientific standpoint, an initial modeling effort helps indicate areas where we do not have complete knowledge. Certain aspects of the modeling estimates are clearly inaccurate. Dysphoria seems more active at the end stages than we have predicted, for example. This may mean that our sample size is not large enough, or (more likely) that our model is overly simplistic and does not recognize, for example, sadness at the ending of analysis.

We also note that there is a wide field of mathematical tools that could be employed to help hone our study, including sensitivity analysis (determining which processes are the most sensitive to perturbations), uncertainty quantification (measuring the propagation of inherent uncertainty in measurements, estimates, and model details), and more detailed dynamical systems approaches to the modeling efforts. Each of these would be likely to add more sophisticated understanding of the process of change in psychoanalysis.

Collaborating with an applied mathematician

We should note that, in the climate of interdisciplinary research, many applied mathematicians are actively interested when an experimentalist or clinician comes armed with data, hypotheses, and questions. "Modeling" is generally accepted as a part of the work of many applied mathematicians and best undertaken with an aim that is outlined by a practitioner who can anchor the project. Just as a mathematician may only have a vague understanding of the details of the application, the practitioner is under no obligation to pursue higher-level mathematics in order to interact with the mathematician. By discussing the science and helping teach each other the esoteric vocabulary and concepts of different disciplines, together the mathematician and the clinician can create results that have lasting impact, beyond what would be possible if they worked in isolation.

To connect with an applied mathematician, look at mathematics department websites. In universities that have separated applied and pure mathematics, look within the applied programs. Most departments have one or more people specializing in mathematical biology, biomathematics, or mathematical modeling. Send the mathematician a brief description of the data and questions. Almost always there will be an interchange where the two potential collaborators are trying to find overlapping language and understanding. This part may seem very confusing at first. It takes some time for the applied mathematician to become familiar enough with the questions of interest to the content specialist such as a clinician to develop any thought of a model. The most important thing that the content specialist can provide is an indication of important features of the data and/or theory that might not be evident, feedback about which questions being addressed are most important to the field, and whether the model's capabilities are useful (i.e., can the model predict something useful? Is there a way to validate the model?). Occasionally a mathematician will move the theory past where the content specialist is comfortable. One should have extreme patience with this – it can sometimes lead to interesting contributions, and is seldom of lasting harm!

Notes

1 We also considered changes in patients who dropped out and patients with negative therapeutic reactions. Insight remained unchanging in these two groups, as did Psychological Health, Paranoid Personality Disorder, and Dysthymia Trait Scale scores.
2 In earlier chapters, we have used the percent of the maximum Insight score.

References

Ablon, J. A., & Jones, E. E. (1999). Psychotherapy process in the National Institute of Mental Health Treatment of Depression Collaborative Research Program. *Journal of Consulting and Clinical Psychology, 67(1)*, 64–75.

Ash, M. G. (1998). *Gestalt psychology in German culture, 1890–1967: Holism and the quest for objectivity*. London: Cambridge University Press.

Beck, A. T., Baruch, E., Balter, J. M., Steer, R. A., & Warman, D. M. (2004). A new instrument for measuring insight: the Beck Cognitive Insight Scale. *Schizophrenia Research, 68*, 319–329.

Birchwood, M., Smith, J., Drury, V., Healy, F. M., & Slad, M. (1994). A self-report insight scale for psychosis: Reliability, validity and sensitivity to change. *Acta Psychiatrica Scandinavica, 89(1)*, 62–67.

Blum, H. P. (1979). The curative and creative aspects of insight. *Journal of the American Psychoanalytic Association, 27*, 41–69.

Connolly, M. B., Crits-Christoph, P., Shelton, R. C., Hollon, S., Kurtz, J., Barber, J. P., et al. (1999). The reliability and validity of a measure of self-understanding of interpersonal patterns. *Journal of Counseling Psychology, 46*, 472–482.

Crits-Christoph, P., Barber, J. P., Miller, N. E., & Beebe, K. (1993). Evaluating insight. In N. E. Miller, L. Luborsky, J. P. Barber, & J. P. Docherty (Eds.), *Psychodynamic treatment research: A handbook for clinical practice*. New York: Basic Books, pp. 407–422.

Cromer, T. D., & Hilsenroth, M. J. (2010). Patient personality and outcome in short-term psychodynamic psychotherapy. *Journal of Nervous and Mental Disease, 198*, 59–66.

Diemer, R. A., Lobell, L. K., Vivino, B. L., & Hill, C. E. (1996). Comparison of dream interpretation, event interpretation, and unstructured sessions in brief therapy. *Journal of Counseling Psychology, 43(1)*, 99–112.

Edelstein-Keshet, L. (1988). *Mathematical models in biology.* Philadelphia: Siam.

Fenichel, O. (1941). *Problems of psychoanalytic technique* (D. Brunswick, transl.). Albany, NY: The Psychoanalytic Quarterly.

Fisher, S., & Greenberg, R. P. (1977). The mechanisms of psychoanalytic therapy: The search for insight. In *The scientific credibility of Freud's theories and therapy.* New York: Basic Books, pp. 346–391.

Freud, S. (1913). On beginning the treatment. In J. Strachey (Ed. and transl.), *The standard edition of the complete psychological works of Sigmund Freud* (Vol. 12). London: Hogarth Press, pp. 121–144. (Reprinted in 1981.)

Gelso, C. J., Kivlighan, D. M., Wine, B., Jones, A., & Friedman, S. C. (1997). Transference, insight, and the course of time-limited therapy. *Journal of Counseling Psychology, 44(2),* 209–217.

Grande, T., Rudolf, G., Oberbracht, C., & Pauli-Magnus, C. (2003). Progressive changes in patients' lives after psychotherapy: Which treatment effects support them? *Psychotherapy Research, 13(1),* 43–58.

Greenson, R. (1967). *The technique and practice of psychoanalysis.* New York: International Universities Press.

Grosse Holtforth, M., Castonguay, L. G., Boswell, J. F., Kakouros, A. A., & Borkovec, T. D. (2006). Insight in cognitive behavioral therapy. In L. G. Castonguay & C. E. Hill (Eds.), *Insight in psychotherapy.* Washington, D. C.: American Psychological Association, pp. 57–80.

Grossman, D. (1951). The construction and validation of two insight inventories. *Journal of Consulting Psychology, 15,* 109–114.

Hoglend, P., Engelstad, V., Sorbye, O., Heyerdahl, O., & Amlo, S. (1994). The role of insight in exploratory psychodynamic psychotherapy. *British Journal of Medical Psychology, 67,* 305–317.

Hohage, R., & Kubler, J. C. (1988). The Emotional Insight Rating Scale. In H. Dahl, H. Kachele, & H. Thoma (Eds.), *Psychoanalytic process research studies.* New York: Springer-Verlag, pp. 243–256.

Johansson, P., & Hoglend, P., Ulberg, R., Amlo, S., Marble, A., Bogwald, K.-P., Sorbye, O., Sjaastad, M. C., & Heyerdahl, O. (2010). The mediating role of insight for long-term improvements in psychodynamic therapy. *Journal of Consulting and Clinical Psychology, 78(3),* 438–448.

Jones, E. E., Parke, L. A., & Pulos, S. M. (1992). How therapy is conducted in the private consulting room: A multidimensional description of brief psychodynamic treatments. *Psychotherapy Research 2(1),* 16–30.

Kallestad, H., Valen, J., McCullough, L., Svartberg, M., Hoglend, P., & Stiles, T. C. (2010). The relationship between insight gained during therapy and long-term outcome in short-term dynamic psychotherapy and cognitive therapy for cluster C personality disorders. *Psychotherapy Research, 20(5),* 526–534.

Kivlighan, D. M., Jr., Multon, K. D., & Patton, M. J. (2000). Insight and symptom reduction in time-limited psychoanalytic counseling. *Journal of Counseling Psychology, 47(1),* 50–59.

Kohler, W. (1925). *The mentality of apes.* (E. Winter, transl.) New York: Vintage. (Reprinted in 1959)

Kris, E. (1956). On some vicissitudes of insight in psycho-analysis. *International Journal of Psychoanalysis, 37,* 445–455.

Lehman, M. E., & Hilsenroth, M. J. (2011). Evaluating psychological insight in a clinical sample using the Shedler–Westen Assessment Procedure. *The Journal of Nervous and Mental Disease, 199(5),* 354–359.

McCallum, M., & Piper, W. E. (1990). The Psychological Mindedness Assessment Procedure. *Psychological Assessment: A Journal of Consulting and Clinical Psychology, 2(4),* 412–418.

McCullough, L., Kuhn, N., Andrews, S., Valen, J., Hatch, D., & Osimo, F. (2004). The reliability of the Achievement of Therapeutic Objectives Scale: A research and teaching tool for brief psychotherapy. *Journal of Brief Therapy, 2(2),* 72–90.

O'Connor, L. E., Edelstein, S., Berry, J. W., & Weiss, J. (1994). Changes in the patient's level of insight in brief psychotherapy: Two pilot studies. *Psychotherapy, 31(3),* 533–544.

Raskin, N. J. (1949). An analysis of six parallel studies of the therapeutic process. *Journal of Consulting Psychology, 13(3),* 206–220.

Reid, J., & Finesinger, J. E. (1952). The role of insight in psychotherapy. *American Journal of Psychiatry, 108,* 726–734.

Rosenbaum, M., Friedlander, J., & Kaplan, S. M. (1956). Evaluation of results of psychotherapy. *Psychosomatic Medicine, 18(2),* 113–132.

Sandell, R. (1987). Assessing the effects of psychotherapy: II. A procedure for direct rating of therapeutic change. *Psychotherapy and Psychosomatics, 47,* 37–43.

Sandler, J., Dare, C., & Holder, A. (1973). *The patient and the analyst: The basis of the psychoanalytic process.* Madison, CT: International Universities Press.

Sargent, H. (1944). An experimental application of projective principles to a paper and pencil personality test. *Psychological Monographs, 5,* 1–57.

Sargent, H. (1953). *The insight test.* New York: Grune & Stratton.

Shedler, J. (2009). *Guide to SWAP-200 Interpretation.* Unpublished manuscript, Department of Psychiatry, University of Colorado Denver School of Medicine, Aurora, Colorado.

Todes, D. P. (2014). *Ivan Pavlov: A Russian life in science.* New York: Oxford University Press.

Volterra, V. (1928). Variations and fluctuations of the number of individuals in animal-species living together. (M. Wells, transl.) *Journal du Conseil/Conseil Permanent International pour l'Exploration de la Mer,* 3(1), 3–51.

Zilboorg, G. (1952). The emotional problem and the therapeutic role of insight. *The Psychoanalytic Quarterly, 21,* 1–24.

Part IV

Conclusions

Chapter 12

What we have learned with N. G. Cogan

> Our aim will not be to rub off every peculiarity of human character for the sake of a schematic "normality," nor yet to demand that the person who has been "thoroughly analyzed" shall feel no passions and develop no internal conflicts. The business of the analysis is to secure the best possible psychological conditions for the functions of the ego; with that it has discharged its task.
>
> (Freud, 1937/1981)

It has been recognized since psychoanalysis began that the "talking therapy" has a range of outcomes. As psychotherapy developed, it became clear that it too has a range of outcomes, as would also be expected. This longitudinal project sheds light on the question of what characteristics at the beginning of psychoanalysis predict different outcomes. Interestingly, the majority of the significant predictors of the outcomes were single Shedler–Westen Assessment Procedure (SWAP-200) items rather than SWAP-200 personality disorder or trait scale scores. The project provides descriptions of the demographic and personality characteristics of the patients with the different outcomes as the analyses began and as they ended. The project also sheds some light on the place of insight in change during psychoanalysis and of the proportional durations of the three phases of analysis.

As the analyses began

The analysands in this longitudinal study are likely to be similar to analysands beginning analysis in the United States at this time. That is, they were most often White, non-Hispanic men and women in their mid-30s. They were generally well educated. More than 90% were viewed as anxious and/or depressed and 85% were viewed as having a personality disorder. More than 70% had been in mental health treatment before they began analysis and half were on psychotropic medication (most often an antidepressant) as the analysis began. In spite of having problems, they were viewed as being conscientious and ethical, with a sense of humor, and as empathic and likeable as well as self-critical, guilty, and unhappy. They were seen as functioning adequately, with Global Assessment of Functioning (GAF) and Psychological Health Scale scores above 65 and Insight Scale scores at 60% of the maximum possible score.

The analysts are also a rather representative sample of psychoanalysts in the United States. They were generally White, non-Hispanic men and women in private practice. They were not beginners in their professions, which varied. They generally had more than 20 years of professional experience and more than 10 years of psychoanalytic experience. Almost half were "theoretical purists," endorsing only one primary theoretical orientation. The theoretical orientations the analysts endorsed were most often ego psychology, drive/conflict theory, or object relations views. Although the theoretical views of analysts can be a matter of intense discussion and debate, the theoretical views of the analysts of patients in the five outcome groups did not differ.

The analyses were most often four times a week, but included 20% that were three times a week and 8% that were five times a week. Although the frequency of analytic sessions can also be a matter of intense discussion and debate, the outcome groups did not differ in terms of whether the frequency was three, four, or five sessions a week. The analysands were "on the couch" in 85% of the analyses. The fees, in terms of the percentage of the analyst's full fee, varied.

Five outcomes of psychoanalysis

A negative therapeutic reaction

Three of the 60 patients in the study developed a negative therapeutic reaction. Our review of the literature showed that the rate of occurrence of this difficult outcome is the same in psychoanalysis and psychotherapy. Perhaps because they are not frequent, negative therapeutic reactions are not often considered in the outcome literatures of either psychoanalysis or psychotherapy. Although they are not frequent, negative therapeutic reactions are important to recognize, understand, and try to prevent.

As analysis began, the patients who developed a negative therapeutic reaction tended to be viewed as more arrogant than other patients. They also tended to lack close friendships. They were lower than others on a sense of self-importance and, interestingly, higher than others on an item concerning a *lack* of social relationships. They were also more paranoid, more schizoid, and lower in insight than others (Figure 12.1).

The SWAP-drawn picture of the patients as the analyses began is vivid and helpful. Being self-critical was a common description of all of the patients as they began psychoanalysis. However, being viewed as arrogant and lacking close friendships was not at all typical of the 60 patients as they began psychoanalysis.

The patients who developed a negative therapeutic reaction were in analysis for an average of 20.7 months (sd = 8.3). As the analyses ended, they tended to be viewed as feeling inadequate, inferior, or like a failure. They also tended to

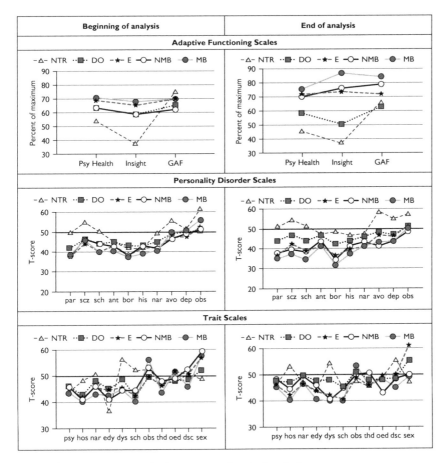

Figure 12.1 Five groups at the beginning and end of analysis

NTR, negative therapeutic reaction; DO, dropped out; E, external events; NMB, no maximum benefit; MB, maximum benefit.

Adaptive Functioning Scales: Psychological Health, Insight, Global Assessment of Functioning (GAF).

Personality Disorder Scales: Paranoid, Schizoid, Schizotypal, Antisocial, Borderline, Histrionic, Narcissistic, Avoidant, Dependent, and Obsessive.

Trait Scales: Psychopathy, Hostility, Narcissism, Emotional Dysregulation, Dysphoria, Schizoid Orientation, Obsessionality, Thought Disorder, Oedipal Conflict, Dissociation, and Sexual Conflict.

be viewed as angry or hostile, as having trouble expressing anger, and as being critical of others. They tended to blame others for their problems more than other patients and to feel that life had no meaning. At the same time, they had higher scores than others on the Avoidant Personality Disorder Scale and lower scores on the Psychological Health Scale. It is not surprising that their Insight Scale scores had not increased over the course of analysis.

The analysts of the three patients ending with a negative therapeutic reaction had less psychoanalytic experience than other analysts (2.7 years [SD = 2.3] vs. 10.9 years [SD = 10.9]). Although this difference was only marginally significant statistically, it will be worth further exploration. Analytic experience might be involved. On the other hand, it seems quite possible that early in psychoanalytic work analysts may be less cautious about taking people into analysis than they are when they have more experience. We are reminded of Wallerstein's note (2002, 2003), described in Chapter 4, that two of his early cases had negative therapeutic reactions.

The present data suggest that, when individuals seek out psychoanalysis, if they seem extremely arrogant or if they seem more arrogant than most people beginning analysis and also seem to lack close friendships, the analyst will most reasonably proceed with considerable caution. With these two items as the analyses began, we successfully predicted all three of the patients who had a negative therapeutic reaction. It is possible that psychotherapy may be the treatment of choice (Gottdiener, 2006), that the analyst might proceed with caution, perhaps in a modified psychoanalysis, or that the analyst might seek consultation from a colleague or group with experience treating more regressed patients.

Dropouts

Twenty-three of the 60 patients in the study dropped out of analysis. Interestingly, our review of the literature showed that the rate of occurrence of dropping out of treatment is similar in psychoanalysis and psychotherapy. As the analyses began, the patients who dropped out tended to be viewed as feeling like an outcast or outsider and had modest but higher scores than others on having an exaggerated sense of self-importance.

The patients who dropped out were in analysis for an average of 26.2 months (SD = 26.6). As the analyses ended, they were anxious, less able than others to be able to form close and lasting friendships, more extremely identified with a social or political "cause," and had less insight into their own motives than others. As the analyses ended, they had higher scores than others on the Paranoid Personality Disorder Scale and lower scores on the GAF and Insight Scales.

We also compared patients who dropped out early and patients who dropped out late in analysis. Six patients dropped out in the first 6 months of analysis. Six patients dropped out after several years of analysis. At the beginning of analysis, patients who dropped out early were more likely than other patients to be viewed as tending to get drawn into abusive relationships. At the beginning of analysis, patients who dropped out after several years of analysis had higher scores than others on having chaotic interpersonal relationships and tending to lie or mislead. Six months before patients dropped out late in analysis, they tended to be viewed as convincing others of their commitment to change and reverting back to maladaptive behavior and tended more than others to become delusional under stress.

The data suggest that when individuals seem to feel like an outcast or out-sider and seem to have a somewhat exaggerated sense of self-importance as they begin psychoanalysis, or when they have tended to be drawn into abu-sive relationships, they are at a significant risk of dropping out of treatment. With the first two items as the analyses began, we successfully predicted 18 of the 23 patients (78%) who dropped out of analysis. Having a history of being drawn into abusive relationships characterized the analysands who dropped out in the first 6 months of analysis. As the analyses began, having a history of abusive relationships was viewed as extremely characteristic of 3 more of the patients who dropped out of analysis for a total hit rate of 21 of the 23 patients (91%). Although on the average patients who dropped out were in analysis for more than 2 years before they dropped out, their insight decreased somewhat, as can be seen in Figure 12.1. The experience of feel-ing like an outcast or outsider, feeling self-important, or having a history of abusive relationships is very likely to be reflected in the transference relation-ship and each will be important to analyze as the patient struggles with ideas of dropping out of treatment.

External factors

Seventeen of the 60 patients in the study ended analysis because of external factors. The patients who ended analysis because of external factors were in analysis for an average of 24.8 months (sd = 19.9). As the analyses began, the patients whose analyses ended because of external factors did not differ from other patients. As the analyses ended, they were viewed as conscientious and responsible and as articulate. They were less likely than others to see their own unacceptable feelings or impulses in others instead of themselves and tended to be more energetic and outgoing than others.

The data show that ending analysis because of external factors is indeed a separate and distinctive way that analyses end. The analysands are noticeably different at the end of analysis from patients who have dropped out.

Without maximum benefits

Six of the 60 analyses in the study ended with mutual agreement between patient and analyst but without maximum benefits. As the analyses began, the patients who ended analysis without maximum benefits were characterized as being more suggestible than others, with work lives that were more chaotic or unstable than was characteristic of other patients. As the analyses began, they were somewhat less likely to be on the couch than others.

The patients who ended analysis with mutual agreement between patient and analyst but without maximum benefits had been in analysis for an average of 55.2 months (sd = 23.0) when the analysis ended. As the analyses ended, they were characterized as appreciating and responding to humor, being able to sustain a meaningful love relationship, and as enjoying challenges. They tended to seek thrills more than others.

When we considered being viewed as more suggestible than others, with much more chaotic or unstable work lives than others at the beginning of analysis, we successfully predicted five of the six analyses (83%) ending without maximum benefits. With just these items, we predicted that one of the six would end with maximum benefits. In all six cases, we predicted that the analyses would end with mutual agreement between patients and analysts.

With maximum benefits

Eleven of the 60 analyses in the study ended with mutual agreement between patient and analyst and with maximum benefits. As the analyses began, the patients who ended analysis with maximum benefits were viewed as being more concerned with rules, procedures, and schedules than others. They had somewhat lower scores than others on the Antisocial Personality Disorder and Narcissism Trait Scales and somewhat higher scores on the Obsessiveness Trait Scale. As the analyses began, they did not differ from other patients on the three adaptive functioning scale scores (Psychological Health Scale, Insight Scale, or GAF scores).

The patients who ended analysis with maximum benefits had been in analysis for an average of 62.0 months (SD = 24.9; range = 28–121 months). As the analyses ended, they were viewed as being psychologically insightful and articulate. Their Insight Scale and GAF scores had increased significantly over the course of analysis. They appeared to have come to terms with painful experiences from the past and to have found meaning in and grown from such experiences, and had lower scores than others on the Paranoid Personality Disorder Scale and higher scores on the GAF scale. In a direct comparison, patients who ended analysis with maximum benefits had higher scores on having moral and ethical standards and trying to live up to them than patients who ended analysis without maximum benefits.

The present data suggest that, when someone seeks out psychoanalysis, being concerned with rules, procedures, and schedules is a positive predictor of an analysis with maximum benefits. This is actually not surprising given that working out the logistics of meeting with an analyst several times a week for what is likely to be a long time is realistically complicated. The concern with rules, procedures, and schedules in the context of beginning analysis may reflect a high level of motivation for analysis. When this item was at least somewhat characteristic of the patient beginning analysis, we successfully predicted seven of the 11 patients (64%) who had maximum benefits from analysis. We predicted that one patient would end without maximum benefits and could make no prediction for three patients. When we considered analyses ending with the mutual agreement of patient and analyst – both successful endings – with and without maximum benefits, we successfully predicted 14 of the 17 outcomes (82%).

Two final notes

The relevant items were not always extremely characteristic of the patient beginning analysis.

The patients who ended analysis with a negative therapeutic reaction, for instance, were *moderately* characterized as arrogant, in contrast with other patients who were scarcely characterized as arrogant at all (with average scores of 4.3 in the index group and 0.6 in other patients). Similarly, patients who ended analysis with maximum benefits were *moderately* concerned with rules, procedures, and schedules, in contrast to other patients (with average scores of 3.8 in the index group and 1.6 in other patients) but were not, for example, characterized as arrogant, or feeling like an outsider, items that were predictors of other outcomes.

Setting aside the 17 analyses interrupted because of external events, we were successfully able to predict 77% of the outcomes of the 43 analysis. If analyses ending with mutual agreement between patient and analyst with or without maximum benefits are combined, we were successfully able to predict 81% of the outcomes.

Finally, the reader may recall that several analyses are still under way. The average length of these analyses is approaching 6 years. We are aware that, as these analyses come to a natural end, the proportions of the outcome categories will necessarily change. Analyses, as the reader knows, can sometimes continue for a good number of years. We hope to report on these outcomes in a brief report at a later time.

Insight and change

We have also described a step in the direction of developing a mathematical model for the quantification and prediction of several outcome measures. Our model describes the dynamic behavior of SWAP Insight Scale scores in relation to three other SWAP scale scores – one adaptive functioning scale, one Personality Disorder Scale, and one trait scale – and provided a reasonable (but by no means perfect) fit to the available data. The modeling indicates that changes in the other variables appear to follow changes in insight. This finding supports the important psychoanalytic tenet that insight into oneself leads to positive changes. We have also described how the model provides support for the division of analysis into a relatively short (10% of the total) beginning phase, a substantial middle phase, and a rather long (25% of the total time) termination phase. Ideally this estimate could be refined by additional model analyses, although the general trend is quite evident.

The model described could be viewed as helping support theoretical aspects of analysis (insight leading change) and helping quantify certain aspects of analysis (delineation of phases). From a mathematical standpoint the model is quite crude and clearly the assumptions are too strong; however, this is often the case in an initial modeling effort. With model refinements we would expect to be able to make several other key observations/predictions. In fact, an end goal of the modeling might be the ability to classify (with some reliability) the outcome based on the early stages of analysis. We view this as an extremely important and useful role in modeling since it might help guide the analysis to some extent.

It may be of interest to the reader that mathematicians are very keen on branching into uncharted territory. Bringing tools developed over the past two centuries of grappling with understanding physical, chemical and biological processes, mathematical modelers are often able to make connections and intuitive leaps that are more difficult for those "in the trenches." Moreover, the collaboration between mathematical theorists and clinicians has the potential to benefit both partners. Just as the clinician can benefit from allowing the mathematical theorist to pursue certain avenues, the mathematical theorist gains a new arena to expand into. Mathematical biology is now a generally accepted sub-field in mathematics and there is an accumulating momentum to include psychological studies. At a recent international conference of the Society for Mathematical Biology, an entire session was devoted to modeling in psychology and psychiatry; a paper by Moore (2015) concerned obsessive-compulsive disorder. Just as in the past, most of mathematical theory is developed to answer relatively practical questions such as those outlined in the previous chapters.

Our final comment regarding modeling in general, and this model in particular, is that a model should be viewed as a step toward understanding. One of the ways of judging the utility of a mathematical model is to determine whether we have learned something new and whether we have new questions to ask. Our model points the way to future studies to refine aspects of our observations while lending support for the importance of insight in leading to change in psychoanalysis. As perturbations in insight are reduced and insight slowly but steadily increases, the clinician can recognize the development of the termination phase.

Forward!

We chose to work with the SWAP-200 measure for conceptual and empirical reasons. As we have worked with the measure, our appreciation has continued to grow because the measure is well developed and empirically tested, and because the items are jargon-free and cover a tremendous range of personality characteristics. We suggest that each clinician – each psychoanalyst and each psychotherapist – choose a good clinician report measure such as the SWAP-200 or its revision, the SWAP-II, and complete the measure to describe each long-term patient on a regular schedule – perhaps every 6 months – as part of case notes. Completing the SWAP takes 30–45 minutes the first time it is used but reduces to about 20 minutes after it becomes familiar. The reflection about the patient and the analysis involved in completing the SWAP can itself be useful, as quite a few of the analysts participating in the longitudinal project commented to us during data collection. Noticing changes in the most strongly endorsed items and in the scale scores is quite likely to be useful and is not, in itself, a formidable task.

It seems very possible that a good clinician report measure such as the SWAP-200 or the SWAP-II could be taught and used in psychoanalytic institutes, graduate training programs in psychology, psychiatry residency programs, and clinical social work programs. A good clinician report measure could become part of regular reporting in, for instance, the 6-month summaries of trainees' cases that are required in many training situations. Clinicians could use such a measure for both training and research purposes. A program that incorporated the SWAP in training, might, for instance, choose to replicate our findings.[1] Institutes and other settings quite probably have empirically oriented researchers in their group who might be very willing to help plan and then help work with the resulting data, perhaps with a small team of instructors and/or candidates at the program. This could be done without identifying patients and without intruding on the privacy of the analytic relationships. We can imagine each institute introducing members one by one, coming to the researcher and introducing him or her saying "and this is our researcher." At the same time, the cautionary tale of the grand plan of the American Psychoanalytic Association years ago to pool data from all members, described in Chapter 2, must also be kept in mind (cf. Hamburg et al., 1967).

We are convinced that dropouts would be reduced if analysts, mental health clinicians, or trainees knew of our finding that dropouts tended to feel more like an outcast or outsider, for instance, than other patients. We believe that clinicians given this information might pay somewhat more attention to the salient individual characteristic than they would have without knowing about these findings. Feeling like an outcast or outsider in the transference, for instance, might be noted and might be commented on with more focus than might have otherwise been the case. We would expect that dropouts would be reduced. Similarly, we would expect that knowing that patients who are unusually arrogant and self-important are more likely than other patients to have a negative therapeutic reaction might be clinically useful and make these reactions less frequent. As is always the case, more research is needed.

Endings

We began this book by considering the case of Anna O. in the prehistory of psychoanalysis. We began by recognizing that, before Anna O. became gravely ill, she had cared for her father every night for 5 months with organization and devotion. This resonates with the characteristic that predicted outcomes with maximum benefits in the present work. We are less clear about what Anna O. was like just as the talking therapy ended. But if we skip ahead to the rest of her life, we see that she had, indeed, come to terms with painful experiences from the past and had grown from these. She lived her life with remarkable moral and ethical standards which she expressed in devotion to helping others and in creative work as well. Each reader may certainly have their own view. The cathartic treatment was certainly not psychoanalysis proper. As for us, we doubt that Anna O. would have turned out as well without the talking therapy. We conclude that the characteristics of people beginning psychoanalysis who ended analysis with maximum benefits and the characteristics of Anna O. as she began the talking therapy and as she lived her life are in harmony.

Note

1 The SWAP-II includes the items we found of special value in predicting outcomes.

References

Freud, S. (1937). Analysis terminable and interminable. In J. Strachey (Ed. and transl.), *The standard edition of the complete psychological works of Sigmund Freud* (Vol. 23). London: Hogarth Press, pp. 211–253. (Reprinted in 1981.)

Gottdiener, W. H. (2006). Individual psychodynamic psychotherapy of schizophrenia: Empirical evidence for the practicing clinician. *Psychoanalytic Psychology, 23(3),* 583–589.

Hamburg, D. A., Bibring, G. L., Fisher, C., Stanton, A. H., Wallerstein, R. S., Weinstock, H. I., & Haggard, E. (1967). Report of ad hoc committee on central fact-gathering data of the American Psychoanalytic Association. *Journal of the American Psychoanalytic Association, 14,* 841–861.

Moore, P. (2015). A hierarchical narrative framework for OCD. Paper presented at meetings of the Society for Mathematical Biology, Atlanta, GA.

Wallerstein, R. S. (2002). The generations of psychotherapy research: An overview. In M. Leuzinger-Bohleber & M. Target (Eds.), *Outcomes of psychoanalytic treatment: Perspectives for therapists and researchers.* New York: Brunner-Routledge.

Wallerstein, R. S. (2003). Reconsidering an analytic outcome: Success or failure? In J. Reppen & M. A. Schulman (Eds.), *Failures in psychoanalytic treatment.* Madison, CT: International Universities Press, pp. 121–152.

Index

abusive relationships, and dropouts 72, 146, 147

Adaptive Functioning Scales: and attrition from external factors/dropouts 67, 79, 86–7, 88; at beginning of the project 41; and negative therapeutic reactions 54, 145; and outcomes without maximum benefits 98; outcomes with/without maximum benefits 109, 110, 111, 117, 118; and SWAP-200 33

alcohol problems: and attrition from external factors 50, 64, 77, 95, 99, 107

American Psychoanalytic Association 14, 30, 35, 62

analysands *see also* patient factors: patient factors of 143–4; taking part in the project 37–8, 39–40

analyses: and attrition from external factors 80, 82, 89; characteristics of 39, 40, 42; and dropouts 68, 71, 89; ending with mutual agreement 93, 147–8; and negative therapeutic reactions 53–4, 57, 144; outcomes with maximum benefits 111, 113, 148; and outcomes without maximum benefits 99, 101; outcomes with/without maximum benefits 114, 116, 119–20, 123; with positive outcomes 116; in the project 144

analysis, effectiveness of 117, 123

analysts: and attrition from external factors/dropouts 66–7, 79–80, 88–9; and negative therapeutic reactions 53, 145; and outcomes without maximum benefits 98–9; outcomes with/without maximum

benefits 109, 110, 119; taking part in the project 35–7, 41–2, 144

analytic goals 5–7 *see also* goals; outcomes

analytic treatments, failures in 48

Anna O. 3–4, 5, 8, 127, 151–2

Antisocial Personality Disorder 109, 148

anxiety 50, 63, 77, 95, 107

applied mathematicians, collaborating with 136–7, 150

arrogance 57, 89, 92, 144, 146, 149

assessment, of personality characteristics 31

attrition from dropping out *see* dropouts

attrition from external factors: and analyses 80, 82, 89; and analysts 79–80, 88–9; and dropouts 76, 84, 147; patient factors 76–9, 80–2, 85–8, 89–90, 91, 92; prevalence of 76; reasons for 75

Avoidant Personality Disorder 56, 77, 107, 145

Babyak, M. A. 34

Bachrach, H. M. 15

Baekeland, F. and Lundwall, L. 63, 76

Balint, M. 5–6

Beck, A. T. 7

Beck Depression Inventory (BDI) 22

behavior therapy 7, 50, 94–5, 106–7

Berlin Institute 105

Bernays, Martha 4, 5

Beutel, M. and Rasting, M. 18

Blass, R. B. 7, 124

Blum, H. P. 127

borderline personality disorders, and psychoanalysis 19

www.ingramcontent.com/pod-product-compliance
Ingram Content Group UK Ltd.
Pitfield, Milton Keynes, MK11 3LW, UK
UKHW020350010325
455677UK00021B/376